The New
Guideposts
Treasury of
Faith

The New Guideposts Treasury of

Faith

Compiled by
the Editors

Guideposts®
Carmel, New York

Contents

Preface

We at Guideposts like to think that *Guideposts* magazine is a continuation of the great roll call of faith that begins in the eleventh chapter of the Book of Hebrews. *Guideposts* was begun nearly half a century ago to tell the stories of twentieth-century men and women who live by faith. By faith they have changed lives and circumstances, conquered fear, coped with disasters and dangers, and looked death in the face. In all the circumstances of their lives—ordinary and extraordinary—they have found that exercising faith unleashes tremendous power.

But faith is not a magic wand—a fact demonstrated both in the Bible and in *Guideposts* stories. Faith is trust in God—a God who loves and cares for us, who has promised to be with us and help us, and to direct our lives if we will follow His directions.

Faith in such a God doesn't keep us out of difficulties, but it does take us through the dark and painful times with the certainty of God's presence. It gives us the strength to keep going in what seem to be impossible situations, to work long and hard in the jobs we've been given, and never to give up the dream God has put in our hearts.

Faith learns to praise God, not only for what He has done in the past, both in our own lives and in the lives of others, but also for what He is going to do for us in the future, even though we can't see how He will work.

Faith, like playing the piano, can only be learned by doing. So we invite you to join the people whose stories, which first appeared in *Guideposts* magazine, are included in *The New Guideposts Treasury of Faith.* As you read, we hope you, too, will put your faith into practice and become part of the roll call of faith. Together we will leave a shining legacy for future generations.

—The Editors

Faith Begins
with God

What Is Faith?

Lois Mae Cuhel

It is trust beyond all doubting
In God who rules above!
It is obedience without question.
It is resting in His love.
It is smiling through the teardrops.
It is struggling through each test.
It is the firm belief our Father
Is a God who knoweth best!
It is knowledge He will give us
Light for each step of the way;
Grace for problems we encounter
And strength for each new day.

"When I Consider Thy Heavens"

Arthur Gordon

I once knew a very intelligent man who wrestled mightily with the question of faith. He didn't consider himself a believer, but he wanted to be one. So he listened to sermons and he read books and he studied the works of theologians and he brought all his very considerable intellectual powers to bear, but nothing seemed to make any difference. His mind remained dominated by doubts.

Then one day when I met him he seemed different. Quieter. Happier. Calmer. The change was so apparent that I asked him what brought it about.

He said, "You won't believe how simple it was."

"Yes, I will," I assured him. The causes behind great changes are often very simple.

He told me that his mother lived in one of our southern states and he had been spending some time with her. One day during the visit he fell into conversation with her gardener, an elderly black man named Ambrose, whose face, he said, radiated a remarkable serenity and benevolence . . . "as if he were in love with life and everything in it." When, half joking, my friend asked Ambrose what made him so happy, the old man said that things were always happening that made him happy. The most recent was the recovery of his daughter from an illness that had been pronounced terminal. Indeed, the doctors at the hospital had warned her father that she only had a few hours to live.

The old gardener told my friend that he went home and opened his Bible and read how Hezekiah, the king of Israel, had asked the Lord to spare him when he was on his deathbed. And how the Lord saw his tears and answered his prayer and granted him fifteen more years of life. Ambrose said he got down on his knees with the Bible open on the bed in front of him, and he begged the Lord with tears to grant his daughter fifteen years of life, or even more. And from that moment his child began to make a recovery that left the doctors baffled and amazed. "You see," the old gardener said, "I know prayer works because I believe in God."

"And why do you believe so firmly in God?" my doubting friend asked him.

The old man looked surprised. "Why," he said, "when I gaze

up in the sky and see the sun and the moon and the stars, I know Somebody had to put them up there. That's why I believe in God. Who else could have done it?"

"You know," my friend said to me, "all the books I'd read, all the studying I'd done, left me untouched. Unchanged. But somehow that simple phrase *'Who else could have done it?'* seemed to reach down deep inside me. And something in me, something very quiet, something very profound, was ready at last to accept that old man's answer. *Only God could have done it.*

"Wasn't it the Psalmist who said, 'When I consider thy heavens, the work of thy fingers, the moon and the stars, which thou hast ordained . . .'?" (Psalm 8:3)

He stopped speaking, and I could see that he was deeply moved. Finally he said, "I don't have any doubts anymore, but perhaps I have a word for those who do. Stop wrestling with all those tremendous unanswerables. Just go outside and look up into the night sky and ask yourself who or what could have created such mystery and majesty. Then listen—and perhaps the same answer will come to you that came to me: *Only God could have done it.*

"When you offer that answer to yourself, and really accept it, your doubts will fade away."

God Is Now/Here ह⤳

Editors

The barrier between belief and unbelief can be very thin. A young girl hung a sign over her bed which said:

GOD IS NOWHERE

Because a friend cared enough to take her to church fellowship, the girl's heart opened to God and she committed her life to Christ. That night, with one stroke of her pen, she made this one change in the sign:

GOD IS NOW/HERE

Faith Comes
in Many Ways

Step by Step

Helen Inwood

If I can't give You all my heart,
Lord, please accept a little part
And let Your love transform it till
It yields entirely to Your will.
If I can't give You all my days,
Please work through me in little ways
And let a fragment of Your light
Illuminate my mortal night
Until I gladly give the whole—
All my life and all my soul.

Stranger at My Door

June O'Neill

I'd almost turned the woman away that bleak, rainy day. She was a bent-over, poorly clad woman who had been slowly walking down our street, going from door to door. I was curious because she only had time to say a few words before the door was shut in her face.

The rain had fallen steadily all day. So had my spirits. We had little money, time hung heavily on my hands, and I didn't like living in our temporary cramped old military quarters while my husband was in school. At that time, I was so full of doubts and questions that I had no faith in anything or anybody.

Then the woman knocked on my door.

"Ma'am," she said, trembling with cold, "do you have any housework I can do? I can scrub floors or do most anything. I have hungry children at home and no money—"

"I'm sorry," I stammered. "I wish I could help you but I can't."

"Well, thank you anyway," she said, and turned to go.

I tried to dismiss the woman from my mind but I couldn't. I ran to the door and called to her. "Please come back!" She did, wiping rain from her face.

"Let me make you a sandwich and something hot to drink," I heard myself saying.

"Why, God bless you!" she said. "You're a good Christian woman."

The words startled me. Me—a good Christian woman?

She ate quickly, in the manner of a person who lives with hunger. Then she looked around the room and spotted my pile of ironing waiting to be done. Despite my protests, she began to iron.

I gave her all the money I had in the house—just some change—and candy I had bought for the children. Then we talked—about the things that make the world and its people good and bad.

When she left she thanked me for all I had done for her—me and my cheese sandwich and candy and eighty-three cents.

I watched her begin again her slow measured journey down the street. But she had started me on a journey too.

I returned to my church soon afterward and began the journey toward the faith I now have—a faith that has seen me through many crises and made me more aware of others.

That Saturday Night at Ramapo

Leonard LeSourd

A moment in time: P.M. . . . Sunday . . . May 30, 1948. And more than forty years later that moment is as vivid as if it were yesterday . . .

He peered at me quizzically from behind his coffee cup, then posed the question that was to start a revolution in my life.

"Would you like to join a group of us on a weekend retreat next month?"

I was suddenly wary—and a bit confused. "What do you mean, 'retreat'? I don't 'retreat' from anything."

It was a pompous statement, typical of me in the year 1948. A former Air Corps pilot, I was twenty-eight, single, arrogant. The main reason I had come to this big Fifth Avenue church was because of the Thursday-night dances where I heard you could find an attractive date. Harold Brinig, an older businessman and the leader of this Young Adult Fellowship, along with his wife, Mary, had for some reason taken an interest in me. A look of amusement crossed his face at my statement.

"Let's not call it a retreat then," he said, "but an *advance*. The purpose of this weekend is to have fellowship together away from the world."

The music had started again. I pushed my coffee cup back and got up from the refreshment table. "Let me think about it." Then I turned my attention to a chic young Wall Street secretary who'd just been dancing with me.

Things religious were anathema to me then. To be sure, I had been reared in a Christian home, been taught Christian values, but the religion I'd seen was lifeless. I sought excitement, adventure. Sports, flying, writing were my interests.

Right after the war I'd stashed everything I owned in the trunk of my Studebaker—golf clubs, typewriter, flying togs, Air Corps uniforms, and some new civilian clothes—and traveled up, down, and across the country for a year, searching out old Air Corps buddies, trying ineffectually to write a novel about postwar American life.

It seemed almost ironic that when nothing worked out for me that year I had ended up in New York City going to Thursday-night social events in the basement of historic Marble Collegiate Church. And working as a reporter for a small inspirational magazine called *Guideposts*. What was happening to me?

The irony was intensified when Harold Brinig reported the theme of this particular weekend—*commitment to Jesus Christ*. That smacked of old-time emotional religion.

"I don't think I can make it, Harold. Something has come up."

Harold smiled at me. "I understand, Len. You don't want to be committed to anything at this stage in your life."

"It's not that," I lied. "I have an . . . er, interview I must do that weekend."

"Too bad. While everyone else is out having fun on Memorial Day weekend, you have to work."

Harold was pinning me against the wall and we both knew it. I began to wriggle off. "I'll see if I can change the interview to another time," I said lamely. Harold had been more on-target than he realized. I had just broken my engagement to Debby, a lovely and gifted woman, because I didn't want to commit myself to marriage.

At that point I think I was typical of many males in America— and throughout the world—today. I wanted inner toughness . . . to be strong . . . cool. The *macho* philosophy. I hated to lose my composure. I'd never forgotten my embarrassment when, at the age of thirteen, I'd been out with my friends and I'd cried copious tears while watching a sad movie. Tears, I decided, were a sign of weakness. I gave myself an order: *I will not cry again—ever.*

To obey this order had been costly. A hardening process began, climaxed by three years in World War II. I became a selfish, self-centered, egotistical, spiritually dead person. Frozen on the inside. My arrogance was a front for a starved spirit and a parched soul.

Yet I didn't want to change. To appease that part of me so repelled by the weekend theme of commitment, I said to myself: *It's no big deal. Didn't I make a kind of commitment at age twelve when I joined the Church?*

If Harold Brinig had heard this, he would have chuckled at the self-deception. He and Mary had encountered many recalcitrant individuals like me who had first come to Marble Collegiate Church to further their social life, certainly not wanting a religion that made demands on them.

The truth was that this particular church, located in mid-Manhattan at a crossroads of busy life, had a special mission for its young people's work—to salvage mixed-up lives. The strategy was to attract them first to evenings of fun and dancing, then encourage them to attend Sunday nights for some spiritual substance. Soon they would be coming to church Sunday mornings—if they could find a seat—to draw inspiration from Dr. Norman Vincent Peale.

This was my pattern over a period of weeks. What gradually began to penetrate my thick outer shell was the caring attitude of so many of the young people. I had never felt this kind of *agape* love inside or outside a church.

One clerk-typist with large eyeglasses told me one day she was praying for me.

Startled, I asked, "Why?"

"So you will find fulfillment in your work," she answered with a smile.

I thanked her. It was strangely unsettling, even frightening, but also touching.

So, little by little, I began to change my mind. I decided that I'd go to the "retreat" after all.

Twenty-six of us crowded into cars that Friday afternoon for the two-hour drive from mid-Manhattan across the Hudson River to Ramapo, New York, not far from the New Jersey line. Included were young executives of both sexes, secretaries, typists, an auto mechanic, a tugboat operator, a Wall Street broker, a dress designer, an accountant, an editor, plus assorted students.

On Friday night we forgathered in a spacious lounge at the retreat center for our first meeting. Right away I knew I was in trouble. A young man told of an experience he'd had upon arrival at the retreat center that afternoon. He had gone into the small chapel, knelt at the altar, and prayed that the Lord would melt any cold hearts among the weekend group.

He didn't know it, but he was talking about *my* cold heart. I quickly calculated what would happen if I slipped out of the meeting, grabbed my suitcase, and drove back to New York alone. Then I sighed. If I did that, the people who came with me in my car wouldn't have rides back to the city. Grimly, I hunkered down for a miserable weekend.

By dinnertime Saturday night I had relaxed a bit. There was some fun and sports recreation mixed in with the meetings. To my surprise, Harold Brinig played a strong third base in a softball game. And he was approaching fifty!

As we left the field, Harold put a sweaty hand on my shoulder and with that disarming smile said, "Len, we all love you."

A knot of hardness dissolved inside me. I began giving more of myself to people at mealtimes and between meetings.

After dinner that night an episode occurred that shook me. A few of us were discussing personal honesty in workaday situations. I agreed that taking company property was wrong, but scoffed at the idea that employees should be honest dealing with superiors or co-workers.

"To get ahead you say what the boss wants to hear," I told them.

Merle Wick, an accountant, sharply dissented. "A Christian who lies in situations like that violates his commitment to Christ."

In the discussion that followed I was in a minority. By the time the Saturday-evening meeting began, two opposing forces inside me were in mortal combat.

One side said, *You don't belong here, Len. You don't share the beliefs of these fanatics.*

The other side said, *Your life's a mess, Len. When are you going to do something about it?*

It was the carefully crafted but emotionally frozen person versus an emerging individual who called for a revolution in his nature. During the meeting one person after another described how a life run by Jesus freed them from past bonds. Mary Brinig summed it up by reading this statement of Jesus to His disciples: " 'Ye have not chosen me, but I have chosen you . . . that ye should go and bring forth fruit' " (John 15:16).

"How exciting to think that Christ is choosing each one of us to be a disciple for Him in New York City," she concluded.

The meeting then ended and I escaped out into the night, unaware that people immediately began praying for me. I walked about aimlessly under a starry May sky, my emotions churning, knowing somehow that my feet would take me to the chapel. Finally I opened its door and stepped inside.

It was a simple, crudely furnished room with folding chairs for about twenty. Up front was an altar; behind that a picture of Jesus with outstretched arms.

But the chapel wasn't empty! A young woman sat on one of the chairs praying. Embarrassed to be there, I turned to leave, but my feet wouldn't move. Instead, they took me slowly down the center aisle to the altar.

Inside me a dam was ready to break and I fought to prevent it. *Cool it, Len. Strong men don't cry. Get out of this place and tomorrow you'll be yourself again.*

The other voice said, *Jesus wept. And He is the strongest of all.*

Then the first voice took another tack. *Don't kneel! That's a surrender of your manhood.*

For a long moment I stood there, frozen in time, aware of the shallowness of my self-centered life, hating it, wanting forgiveness for it, seeing a vision of something so much more worthwhile—if I took this next step.

My knees bent. As I knelt I looked up into the face of Jesus and the dam inside me broke. Tears flowed. In a stumbling prayer I gave myself to Him.

When the group met the next day after breakfast, I knew what I had to do. These people who had loved me and prayed for me wanted a report. When I gave it, I wept once again. To my surprise, no one was embarrassed. Instead, my tears washed away more barriers between me and those who were becoming closer to me than any friends I had made in the course of my whole life.

The fascinating twist to my story is this—in the years that followed, a Christ-centered life brought me adventure, challenges, and fulfillment beyond my wildest dreams. During those years there were, of course, painful defeats and low points as well. But when they came and my faith grew shaky, I had one unfailing remedy. I would go back in time to that Saturday night at Ramapo, New York. Once again I felt the love of a church fellowship thawing my hardened heart. Again I knelt before an altar, accepting the forgiveness of Jesus Christ as I recommitted myself to Him.

That compact I made with Jesus back in 1948 is unchangeable and irrevocable, my rock-solid foundation in the shifting sands of life. And with it goes the promise of a marvelous and infinite future.

And to think I could have missed it!

The Adventure Goes On

Charles M. Duke, Jr.

From movies like *The Right Stuff* and *Terms of Endearment*, I've heard a lot of talk again about what happens to us astronauts after we leave the space program. It's well known that some of us have gone into politics and some into business careers. But what *really* has happened to us after coming back to earth again? I can only speak for Charlie Duke, and my story is one that surprises even me.

I've always been driven by one kind of ambition or another. I suppose I aimed for that flight to the moon ever since I was a youngster watching planes soar over our backyard in Lancaster, South Carolina. I know I worked hard to get into the Naval Academy at Annapolis, and studied hard for my masters in astronautics at MIT. For five years I flew as an Air Force fighter and test pilot, and then went through the six years of rigorous training that finally put me on the Apollo 16 moon flight with Ken Mattingly and John Young. In 1972, we drove the lunar rover across the moon's gray dusty surface.

What was life like after that? Was it all an anticlimax? No, not completely, for I just shifted goals. I put all that drive of mine into making some money. In 1975, I launched out into a civilian career by opening a beer distributorship in San Antonio.

I had no doubt that I was on my way to making my first million. Not that I expected it to come easily either. I worked hard, getting up at 5:00 A.M. to get the trucks on the road, staying late to have a drink with the drivers when they returned from their deliveries.

And then, gradually, something went wrong. Not with the business, but with me. I was working as hard as ever, but I was taking no pleasure in it. My drive seemed to dissipate into a restlessness I simply couldn't understand or handle. The fuel had simply gone out of the rocket.

What is it that's bothering me? I kept asking myself, and sometimes I'd catch myself just sitting in my office, drumming my fingers on the desk, staring. Then one day I saw that I was doing just that: drumming my fingers and staring . . . staring at the ring on my left hand . . . my wedding ring . . .

Looking at that ring took me back, back to the early days when I had married the most beautiful girl I'd ever seen. Her name was Dotty. She was a romantic. Even in the hectic days, no matter where or how often we moved from place to place, Dotty always knew how to create a home for us with the romantic's touch of candles burning and good china at dinner, even when I'd joke and say that hot dogs and paper plates were good enough for me. Together Dotty and I had two sons, and we seemed as happy as most couples, despite the schedules that got worse in space training when I could get home only on weekends.

The wedding ring on my left hand . . . It wasn't just Dotty I was thinking about when I sat staring at it. Again and again my ring made me remember something that happened on our moon flight.

It began on the second day. Ken Mattingly, as per NASA regulations, had to remove all metallic objects, including his watch and wedding ring, while performing a special exercise within the capsule. To prevent them from floating away, he put them into a little pouch on the side of the spacecraft. When getting dressed, he found his watch but the wedding ring had disappeared.

We searched the capsule thoroughly and finally gave it up for lost. Seven days later, on our return trip from the moon, we prepared for our space walk.

We put on our space suits and Ken opened the hatch. Tethered to a communication-oxygen line, he floated into space and moved to the rear of our ship to retrieve two film canisters used during lunar orbit. I drifted out behind him, anchoring myself by wedging my boots in the hatch entrance. As I watched Ken work, I was momentarily blinded by the intensity of the sun's reflection from his white suit against the blackness of space.

Suddenly, out of the corner of my eye I caught a flash of gold. I felt certain it was Ken's wedding band, serenely floating out of the hatch. I grabbed for it, missed, and it sailed on, heading into infinity.

"Good-bye wedding ring," I sighed, watching it tumbling and sparkling in the sun. It was heading in Ken's direction but since he was in serious radio discussion with Houston Space Center I didn't want to interfere.

The next moment the ring struck the back of Ken's helmet. In awe I watched it bounce off and float back toward me on the same trajectory. As it passed my face mask, I grabbed it. We were all amazed. The odds for a disc tumbling through space to rebound perfectly off another object are practically zero.

Now I wondered if that odd experience was trying to tell me something. I looked at my own wedding ring. Was it something about my own marriage?

I had to admit it wasn't the best, despite our nice home and car. Dotty seemed to be as restless as I. And often I'd find her depressed. A few times she even mentioned something about "not wanting to live," but not knowing how to deal with that I just shoved it to the back of my mind.

She said I hardly paid attention to her. Well, I was what they call a "good provider" and I tried to be an attentive husband, even though Dotty was always saying that I flirted with women at parties, that I spent too much time away from her and the kids. But it was for her and the kids that I was throwing myself so completely into the beer distributorship, wasn't it?

During this time of transition, something happened to Dotty that I couldn't understand.

Our Episcopal church had a Faith Alive weekend. Our priest said it would be a "spiritual renewal," whatever that meant. But since we were regular church members, we decided to go along.

I don't remember much about the weekend as my mind was more on getting the beer business going. Besides, I had never taken religion seriously. I went to church because it seemed the right thing to do. The Bible to me was a good, moral story, and by the time I went to the moon, I didn't really believe in a Creator. Jesus to me was a good man, a good teacher, but not the Son of God.

However, Dotty had a different reaction to the weekend. "You know, Charlie," she said, "I was impressed that the leaders were just ordinary businessmen and housewives. They talked about Jesus as a real Person."

She had a faraway look in her eyes: "They said that He had answered their prayers."

"Yeah, yeah," I answered, going over beer distribution tally sheets.

She never said a word about it after that. However, over the next few months I noticed a change in Dotty. Instead of complaining about my lack of attention, she seemed more at peace.

Finally, one evening, she shocked me.

"Charlie, I can't depend on you anymore for my needs. I've decided that the only person I can really depend on is God."

I stared at her, not understanding. "What do you mean?" I asked, slightly angry. "You can depend on me. Don't I bring home the paycheck? Don't we have a nice house?"

"That's not what I mean." Softly she tried to explain how she looked to God now, not me, for her strength and fulfillment in life. But I couldn't understand what she was trying to tell me and forgot about our conversation.

It was two and a half years later when I finally did understand what Dotty was trying to say. On that renewal weekend she had turned her life over to God. At that time she had prayed this simple yet desperate prayer: "God, I don't know whether You are real or not. Jesus, I don't know if You are who You say You are. But if You are, I turn my life over to You and ask You to be in control of my life. I've made a mess of it and I don't want to be in charge of it anymore. If You aren't real, then I want to die."

In the months that followed this prayer, God showed His reality to her and she began to find the love and purpose in life that she had been looking for. I began to see changes in her life. I especially noted a change in her attitude toward me. She didn't nag me as much and she quit reminding me of all the times in the past that I had hurt her. This was a miracle in itself because it seemed that she had the memory of an elephant when it came to remembering all the things I had done wrong. What had happened was that she had forgiven me. Later she told me how Jesus had helped change her heart and had removed all her resentment, bitterness, and hurts. She said Jesus had told her she was born again and He had forgiven her for all her past mistakes, and, in order for our marriage to be born again, she had to forgive me.

In the months that followed, Dotty became even more accepting and loving. After years of drifting apart, our marriage was coming together. I couldn't help think about how, in space, that golden wedding ring had come back.

I was so relieved that I even found myself making a few concessions, like promising not to pay attention to other women at parties. I also made an effort to do more with our two sons, and soon I was helping coach their soccer league.

But, though family life had turned for the better, I still suffered that gnawing feeling of frustration in spite of all my successes. My beer distributorship was on its way to making me that million. But, oddly enough, it didn't challenge me anymore. Finally, I sold it.

What was this strange restlessness deep within me?

Then one Sunday at church Dotty and I were approached by a friend of ours, a local surgeon. "Charlie, there's going to be a Bible study retreat at the tennis club in a couple of weeks. They're going to discuss how prophecy applies to current events. Would you and Dotty like to go?"

"Okay," I said, knowing how Dotty enjoyed "religious" things. But I wondered silently, *How can one study the Bible for a whole weekend?*

When that weekend came, we sat around with about twenty other people in easy chairs in a relaxed atmosphere at the tennis ranch not far from our house. It wasn't churchy at all, nothing preachy or condemning.

As we started studying, I was amazed. I was shown passages in the Old Testament that predicted that one day God would reach out to man by coming to live among us. I thought I knew what was in the Bible, but I didn't remember such prophecies.

Others accurately forecast the town in which Jesus was born, the time of His birth, what He would teach, His rejection, His death and resurrection, and that millions among other nations would become His followers while His own people would see their homeland destroyed and be scattered.

I was staggered to see that the prophets also predicted, over twenty-five hundred years ago, that the Jews would return to Palestine. This one had come to pass right before my eyes in newspaper headlines!

When we got into the New Testament, I saw that Jesus' own claims about Himself ruled out the possibility that He was simply a good man. He had to be either God or the biggest liar who ever walked.

Now I faced the question Jesus asked the people of His own day and still asks today, "Who do *you* say that I am?"

I realized suddenly that I faced a critical decision. The words burned before me: "In the beginning was the Word, and the Word was with God, and the Word was God. . . . And the Word was made flesh, and dwelt among us . . ." (John 1: 1, 14).

With these words impressed on my mind and heart, with all the facts before me, I saw that, yes, Jesus is God, come in flesh, and that He loved me so much He died for me on the cross. When I accepted Jesus' statements as true, I heard no angelic music or witnessed no brilliant flashes, but an inner peace did settle in me.

Now the Bible became even more alive to me. On every page I saw that God is involved in the life of everyone. I began to see that He also wanted to direct my life.

Dotty and I started praying about the kind of business He wanted me in. A friend invited me to join him in a real estate venture, and the more we prayed about it the greater peace I had, sensing that this was the direction God was leading me.

And just as He had with Dotty, the Lord began to come into my thoughts, too. "Charlie," He said, "you love money more than you love Me." I sat down and sent my first tithe to support mission work. It seemed as if I sent my love of money with it.

The inner voice spoke again. "Charlie, you don't love Dotty as I want you to." As I drove back and forth to my new business, I listened to Scripture tapes about love. I began to see what it meant for a husband to cherish his wife more than himself. And, as the months went by, a deep love for Dotty welled within me.

This led to our going on a Christian Marriage Encounter weekend. For the first time in fifteen years we started really sharing our feelings: talking, writing letters to each other. We decided that Jesus would be the head of our home. It was no longer a matter of what I or Dotty wanted, but what *He* wanted for our family.

We saw that our relationship was like a triangle with Jesus at the apex and each of us at the lower corners. The closer Dotty and I got to Jesus, the closer we became to each other.

A few months after the Marriage Encounter, I awakened in the middle of the night. Our bedroom seemed flooded with God's presence. I got out of bed, knelt down, and surrendered myself totally to Jesus, giving Him my family, my business, everything.

Life has indeed become thrilling. I have discovered that Jesus is interested in every little detail of my daily life. Though I still have problems, I have found that He helps me through them. I talk with Him just as I talk with my business partners or friends. And my prayers are informal; I simply tell Him how I really feel and I always find that He understands.

I learned that the ambition pushing me all these years was a drive to find God. When I asked Him to come into my life, He not only forgave my past, He gave meaning to that life. I still have ambition but now it's *His* ambition, urging me on to become all that He created me to be.

In the speeches I make today, I tell how I used to say, "I could live for a thousand years and never have an experience like walking on the moon. But now," I add, "I walk everyday with Jesus and nothing has ever been as exciting!"

That walk on the moon lasted three days, but my walk with Jesus will last forever.

When I Said, "Oh, Yes"

Eleanor Turner

I grew up going to Sunday school—because I was sent. I went to Christian Fellowship—because boys were there. After I was married and the children came, I sent them to Sunday school—because I knew they "ought" to go.

While the kids were growing up, I dropped into church occasionally, but church-going wasn't important to me. *God* was. And once in a while, when the children were very ill or something frightening happened, I'd call Him. But otherwise, I was busy with everyday things.

Then one day, an inspirational magazine turned up in my mail in error; it should have been delivered to Bill Eckert's wife, who lives on our street. Before taking it to her, I read it. I liked it and sent in a subscription. Shortly after that—I'm not sure if the magazine had anything to do with it—I started going to church pretty regularly. I turned it into a kind of challenge. I'd think, *I've gone three Sundays in a row, maybe I can make it four.* Later my husband, Fred, started going with me; I'm not sure when.

One afternoon I was bicycle riding with my neighbor, Betty Rousseau, and we somehow got talking about prayer. She told me about her prayer group. They met at various homes, and prayed for anything and everything. Nothing seemed to be too unimportant or too difficult for them to pray about. Betty asked me if I'd like to go to a meeting. I said, "Sure." The women sang a lot, chatted and prayed a lot. Everyone seemed very caring and I felt at home.

Then one day someone in the group asked me if I wanted to accept Jesus as my Savior and Lord of my life. I didn't really know what she was talking about, but the group was listening for my answer and seemed very anxious that I say "Yes." So to be agreeable, I nodded my head and she prayed a little prayer asking Jesus to come into my life. Everyone was very excited and happy for me.

I soon forgot the little prayer, but later at another meeting, a different woman asked me the same question about accepting Jesus. Again I agreed, and bowed my head for the prayer. And again I forgot about it.

Then one day I was having lunch with another group member and she asked, "Ellie, do you want to invite Jesus to come into your life?" And this time something deep in me said, "Oh, yes."

She said that simple little prayer thanking Jesus for being my Savior and asking Him to forgive me for my sins and to come into my life.

And, strange as it may seem, He really did! He came into my life and with Him came a peace and love I'd never known before. I can't explain it. All I know is something wonderful happened.

Naturally I wish I could have talked more meaningfully with my children about Jesus and how He loves each one of us and stands waiting to be invited into our lives. I wish I could have prayed that little "welcome" prayer with them while they were young, with open hearts.

But maybe God has a special plan for them, all hand-tailored. And when, deep inside, they are ready to say, "Oh, yes," maybe someone will be nearby to pray the little prayer with them.

Maybe you.

The Kind of Fool I Am

David Brian

One night a long time ago a very unimportant thing happened to me. I'm still surprised that I remember the incident at all, for it had so little to do with my life at the time. The moment came and went so quickly that I should have forgotten it, yet out of the millions of seconds of my life I chose to record it.

I was in a New York barroom on a raw, drizzly night during World War II. At that time I was serving in the Coast Guard, a boatswain's mate on forty-eight-hour liberty. New York was my hometown and I was back in the familiar haunts of the Times Square theater district. In fact, I was standing at the long bar of the old Hotel Lincoln, just across the street from the Imperial Theatre where I'd had my first show business job singing in the chorus of New Moon.

The bar was busy. There was a buzz of conversation, sharp clinks of ice, abrupt laughter, when suddenly there came a knocking. At first those of us in the bar could not figure where it came from. But gradually our eyes found him—a man framed in the window, standing outside. When he had our attention, with the gesture of a mime he pointed to a scroll hanging on a string around his neck and resting on his chest. Suddenly he flicked it, letting it unfurl for us to read.

"I am a fool for Jesus," the scroll said. "What are you a fool for?"

He smiled, tipped his hat, bowed, and disappeared. That was all there was to it. He didn't come in to distribute tracts or beg; he just smiled and left.

A few people laughed. Someone said, "Crackpot!" But most of us merely shrugged and returned to our drinks.

For years after that night I never once thought about the man in the window. Then one day the "fool" simply popped into mind, pure and vivid, as though I had seen him only seconds before. In the meantime a lot had happened to me—out of the Coast Guard and back to the theater, from the New York stage to the movies in Hollywood (the eight years as *Mr. District Attorney* were to come later).

In the early 1950s Adrian Booth and I were married, a marriage in which for the first three years we drank too much and quarreled too often. Before any split occurred, however, came the supreme event of both our lives. First Adrian, then I, found Jesus. Everything changed. The course of our marriage was recharted and as we prayed together and gave ourselves to Him, the drinking stopped, the quarreling eased, we began to feel a richness in living.

What caused me to think of the man in the window after so long a time was another stranger, a woman who came up to Adrian and me in a restaurant. Adrian and I always bow our heads and say grace before eating, though in public places we do try not to make a production of it. Still, that evening that woman noticed us and came over.

"I wish I had the courage to do what you did," she said, "to say grace in public. I want to, but I feel a little foolish."

"Well," I said gently, "I guess I'm what is called 'a fool for Jesus.'"

It was the first time I'd ever thought it, much less said it, and it rather startled me. Of course, that's when I thought back to the man in the window—and since then he has become like an old friend. That evening I got a new look at myself. Was I really a fool for Jesus? A crackpot?

I couldn't answer about the crackpot, but it didn't seem to matter, for I had a new warm, proud feeling that perhaps I was indeed a fool for the Lord. As the question, "What are *you* a fool for?" began to repeat itself in my head, I thought about all the extreme things we pursue that make us seem foolish. I thought about how some of us make fools of ourselves for money and drink and drugs and all sorts of rabid enthusiasms, such as buying things and going bananas over sports events. How preferable it seemed to have a passion for Jesus!

After all, in our terms, Jesus had been something of a fool Himself. He'd done some pretty wild, far-out things—healing people, calming storms, giving up His life when He didn't have to. He had done some far-out things for me too—curing an alcohol problem, for one. From the very moment I had given myself to Him, the desire to drink had vanished.

On that historic Sunday morning of my conversion, I had been waiting for the Red Roost to open—that was the bar down the hill from our home—but I never got there. So total was the change that even years later, on a *Mr. District Attorney* personal appearance tour in Cincinnati, when a waiter inadvertently put some gin in the plain tonic water I had ordered, one swallow of it made me physically ill. Why shouldn't I be a fool for Someone who could do that for me?

That moment in the Hotel Lincoln bar had seemed so unimportant, yet it survived in this sieve I call my memory for a significant reason. It's part of the excitement of being one of His followers. You find out that He'll go to any length to get your attention, even to the point of holding up signs.

I'm a fool for Jesus. What are *you* a fool for?

The Greatest Journey Yet

Barry Mayson

You might wonder how a man like me, with a mother and an upbringing like mine, could ever get involved with anything as vicious as the Hell's Angels.

For years I had gone dutifully to Sunday school and listened to my mother talk about God and how He loved us. That sounded right to me until I was sixteen and my stepdad, a man I loved a lot, caught malaria overseas while flying for an international airline. I prayed and asked the Lord to let him live, but he died. His death hit me hard, really hard, and I decided that if God allowed such terrible things to happen, then I wasn't going to have anything more to do with Him. My mother tried to change my mind. But I told her to keep all that Bible stuff.

It seemed to me that the guys who were having fun did all the things Mother had warned me not to do. I began to get a new set of friends, and when my mother learned about the kind of guys I was running with and said she'd pray for me every day, I laughed.

Only one thing really fascinated me: the rough and tough life of bikers. By the time I was twenty-two, I had joined a motorcycle club in Charleston, South Carolina. We supported our rough, vagabond life-style through gambling, drug dealing, and other vices; we protected it with violence. Before long the Hell's Angels, the most brutal motorcycle gang of all, took us into their national network.

Through terror and intimidation the Angels always got what they wanted; their black leather jackets and loud bikes had become a symbol of crime, an object of fear across the country.

It used to surprise me that my mother didn't disown me. I knew she hated everything about my life, but whenever I'd roar up to her door to cadge a shower or crash for the night, she welcomed me.

She still said she never stopped praying for me. "Turn back to Jesus," she'd beg again and again. "It's not too late. Confess your sins. His mighty forces will help you find what you *really* want."

I'd grin as I mounted my bike. "Ma, there ain't nothing mightier than the Hell's Angels!" Laughing, I'd do a wheelie as I spun out of her yard.

The years went by. Even my marriage to Fran didn't keep me off the road. And then one night I ran into trouble. At a Hell's Angels meeting in San Mateo, California, one of our leaders, a man called Wolf, was blowing his top about a rival gang leader in South Carolina.

"I want him dead," he snarled at me. "You're in charge of South Carolina. You take care of it!"

I had bloodied men in fights, slashed faces, and gouged eyes. But murder a man? Maybe it was those Sunday school days that made me say it, I don't know, but I stood up to Wolf. "I'm a Hell's Angel," I told him, "but I'm no murderer."

From that moment on, I was on the Hell's Angels' death list.

That very night I discovered that they were out to get me. I raced up to San Francisco. I needed to get out of California, but I didn't have the money for a plane ticket. I didn't dare ask any of my so-called friends. They might turn me over to the Angels. Suddenly the only two people in the world that I could trust were my wife and my mother, who were both together with my baby daughter in my mother's house in South Carolina.

My mother answered the phone. "Yes, of course," she said. "I'll wire you the money." Then I cowered all night in a cheap hotel room waiting for the Western Union office to open in the morning.

At 9:00 A.M. I headed for the telegraph office. Suddenly, staring at me from across the street was a big blond man with a red beard. I had seen him before. He was a Hell's Angel. Two other leather-jacketed guys were with him. He nudged one, pointed to me, and the three of them headed across the street.

I pushed through the crowd, searching for the Western Union sign, and then . . . ahead, two more faces glared at me. They signaled to the men behind me. They were closing in on me.

I rushed on, panting, my knees wobbling. A red neon cafeteria sign flashed in front of me and I ducked inside. I headed for the rear where pay phones lined a wall. I had to call those two women at home. I had to tell them that I loved them, before those guys grabbed me.

I dialed Mother's number and told the operator that Barry Mayson was calling collect. *Someone answer, please!*

"Hello?" It was Fran.

"Hey, baby," I choked.

"Where are you? We've been worried!"

My throat swelled. "Baby," I whispered, "I just wanted to tell you . . . how much I love you." I blinked back tears. "I'm sorry for the way I've treated you and Mother . . . can you forgive me?"

"Yes, Barry, yes!"

I glanced over my shoulder. Two of the Angels had come into the cafeteria; the others had grouped outside.

My hands turned icy. "The Hell's Angels are after me," I whispered. "They're right on my back."

"But we sent you money. We'll meet you here at the airport."

"Sweetie, there's no way. They're all around me. I just called to say good-bye." A shadow fell across the phone. I turned; two men were standing behind me.

"We want to use the phone."

I pointed to the others.

"We want *that* phone, man!" snarled the other.

"Well, I'm using it!" I figured as long as I gripped the phone I'd be safe. It would make too much of a ruckus for them to drag me out while I held on to the receiver. I was right. They stepped back.

My mother's voice came on. "Son, I've been listening on the extension. Now listen, everything's going to be all right."

"Mother, you don't understand. These guys are going to kill me. I just want to tell you how sorry I am for the terrible things I have done."

"Son," my mother told me, "I love you. All of those things are forgiven. Barry, listen; there's hope for you."

"Mother, there are two guys here who are about to kill me. What kind of hope could there be?"

"Son, your hope is in Jesus Christ."

I stared down at the cafeteria floor littered with cigarette butts and candy wrappers. "Mother," I said quietly, "Jesus Christ couldn't care for me. When Dad died, I cursed God."

Her voice was gentle, but measured. "Son, it doesn't matter. Jesus loves you. Two thousand years ago He gave His life for you. He shed His blood for you."

Her words swept me years back to my Sunday school classes again. I could see the picture on a classroom wall of Jesus hanging on the cross.

"He died for your sins." My mother's voice was insistent. "All you have to do is ask Him to forgive you and He will."

Would He? Could He? I found myself desperately *wanting* to believe. "Mother, I don't even know how to talk with God."

"It doesn't matter what you say," she said. "I'll pray, and you pray with me."

"All right," I sighed, slumping against the phone.

"Lord Jesus," said Mother, "I know I'm a sinner. I just ask that You forgive me of my sins, come into my heart, and help me live for You."

As I repeated her words, something broke inside of me. I found myself crying. I felt a rush of love. I felt peace and warmth. I *knew.* I knew that Jesus had forgiven me and that He had come into my heart. I could hear Him saying: "I love you. I forgive you for everything." Through the drugs, drinking, and depravity, I had been struggling for some kind of acceptance. Now I'd found it. For the first time in my life I felt free. I glanced behind me. The two Hell's Angels looked puzzled. Bikers don't cry.

The rest of the gang still hung around outside. I got scared all over again as I thought about what would happen as soon as I hung up the phone.

"Mother," I choked, "I know that God loves me and I know that I'm going to be with Him. I just wish I could get home to see you all again."

Now her voice was direct and cool. "There is a way, Barry. Look through the Yellow Pages and find a minister to call."

"Mother, as soon as I hang up these guys will grab me."

"Well, then, look through the book now and give me a number."

With the phone pressed against my shoulder, I started paging through the phone book on its chain. I found the listings marked "Clergy" and looked down the long columns of ministers' names. Which one? Which one? My finger stopped at "Browner, Avery B."* I read off the number.

"All right," Mother said, "Fran will call him from our neighbor's phone right now and tell him to come get you. You stay right there. Don't hang up."

As I waited—another hour, then two, all the while talking with my mother—the two men behind me joined the others outside. I thought of calling the police, but with my record, that seemed just as bad as facing my former "brothers."

My mother kept talking to me. She read from her Bible, John 10:29 (RSV), where Jesus said, "My Father, who has given them to me, is greater than all, and no one is able to snatch them out of the Father's hand."

I glanced at the killers lurking outside. I knew now that God loved and forgave me. But I still wasn't sure of His power.

A tall, husky man in a navy blue suit strode through the cafeteria toward me.

"Are you Barry Mayson?" he asked.

"Who are you?" I replied suspiciously.

"Avery Browner," he said. "Assembly of God. Your wife asked me to come down here. She said you needed help."

"The minister is here," I told my mother. "What now?"

"Son, you have given your life to Jesus. Now you have to trust Him." Then her voice took on a tone I hadn't heard since I was a little boy. "Son, go with that minister now. I'm going to hang up."

I was silent for a moment. Was this that step of faith I used to hear about?

"All right, Mother. Good-bye." Then I turned to the minister. "Well, let's go."

We walked out onto Market Street. The men waiting there backed up. The minister was a big man; the Angels must have thought he was a plainclothes cop. The minister and I stopped and looked at each other.

"What's your problem?" he asked.

"I just quit the Hell's Angels," I said, glancing toward the group, "and these guys are out to kill me."

---

*Name has been changed.

"What do you want me to do?"

"Just walk down to Western Union with me so I can get my money for plane fare out of here."

"I can't do that," he said.

"Why? I thought you guys were supposed to help people in trouble."

"Yes," he said, and then added thoughtfully, "but this is something you must do yourself."

I stared at him, stunned. Yet I could tell there was no use arguing with him. I had already taken that first step of faith by leaving the phone. Now I faced an even rougher one.

I wheeled and started toward Western Union. Out of the corner of my eye I saw the Hell's Angels move along behind me.

"O Lord," I breathed, forcing one foot after the other, "let me get home. Let me get the money and get out of here." I walked faster, trying to mix in with the crowd on the sidewalk. And then I saw the big yellow sign: "Western Union."

I slipped into the door and stepped up to a woman sitting behind a glass partition. "Do you have a moneygram for Charles Barry Mayson?"

She riffled through some papers and asked for my identification. As she counted out the money, I saw two Hell's Angels reflected in the glass; they were standing outside, arms folded.

The lady slid the money under the window to me. As I stuck the bills in my pocket, I vowed that if they got me, I would go kicking and screaming.

The two men flanked me as I walked to the door. *Well, Lord, this is it,* I thought, stepping out onto the street.

As the other Hell's Angels closed in, I looked up. Over one of my attacker's shoulders I could see the bulk of Mr. Browner hurrying toward me. "Hey, man, hey!" I shouted. As he lumbered up, the Angels fell back.

I grabbed Mr. Browner's arm. "Man, I'm glad to see you. They were just fixing to get me!"

He placed beefy hands on my shoulders. "You know, Barry, the Lord seemed to have a reason for my letting you go on alone at first. And then He told me: 'That man is in real trouble and *now* he needs your help.' "

A couple of hours later, I was on a plane bound for South Carolina, and I found myself wondering, *What will happen now? Will my life always be in danger?* But overpowering the fear was the strong assurance that I belonged to Him. When I surrendered to God in that cafeteria, His mighty power *did* come to my aid, just as my mother had promised. As that Scripture guaranteed, no one could snatch me away from Him now.

My window blazed with sunlight. Together we were beginning the greatest journey yet.

The Knock at My Door

Claudia Leaman

At first I didn't listen. Finally I did.

I could hardly believe what my older brother, Hal, was saying to me. His suggestion was ridiculous, absurd—he wanted me to get down on my knees and give my life to Christ! I was shocked and repelled. My brother had become a Jesus freak!

It was the last night of my weekend visit with him in Cambridge, Massachusetts, where he was studying. We were sitting in his apartment, on the roll-away couch that served as my bed, discussing religion. He could not have chosen a touchier subject, for I had recently decided that I was an atheist. I was just eighteen and a few months earlier had started college, leaving home for the first time.

I tried to explain to Hal the way I felt. "Ever since I can remember," I told him, "I've gone to church and Sunday school just because it was the thing to do. But now that I'm in college, I realize that I never thought any of it out for myself. I can't justify my old beliefs to myself or to the kids in the dorm. I think I've been an atheist all along."

"Barb," Hal said slowly, calling me by my family nickname, "God is still there. All you have to do is ask Him into your life."

I had noticed in Hal a new kind of strength and assurance, and I admired that—but then I had always admired Hal. Ever since I was seven and my father died, Hal had been special to me, helping me with my lessons, giving me books to read. Now it seemed that if I couldn't trust Hal, there was no one I could trust.

Hal kept telling me what he thought I should do. Finally, just to please him, I did the last thing I ever pictured doing on a visit to my brother. I went down on my knees and repeated the words he suggested: "Jesus, please come into my life . . ."

Nothing happened. I only felt awkward and embarrassed. After a short while I got up. Hal embraced me and said good night. I was grateful that he didn't ask me how I felt.

When he left the room I began to cry. I cried all night and most of the next day. Because I could no longer understand Hal. Because I was confused and alone.

The next time I saw my brother was a few months later at a family gathering. He made a point of talking to me alone. "How do you feel about accepting Christ into your life?" he asked.

"It may be all right for you," I blurted, "but not for me." Hal could see I didn't want to be questioned about it.

For ten years we dropped the subject, and I tried to put the experience out of my mind. During that time I graduated from college and began my acting career. I fell back into my old, half-understood ways of occasionally going to church. But I never quite knew why, or what I was looking for there.

Early in 1977 I found myself in the rehearsal room of the Ansonia Theater in New York with the director and cast of *Jesus Christ, Superstar.* I had a role as one of Jesus' followers, and we were preparing for a production on Long Island. Five months earlier I had played Sonya, also a follower of Christ, in *Godspell.* Both were very popular musical plays about the life of Jesus Christ and both had hit songs on the radio: the title song and "I Don't Know How to Love Him" from *Superstar,* and "Day by Day" from *Godspell.*

When I got the role in *Superstar,* I promised myself that what had happened to me in *Godspell* wouldn't happen again. Acting in that play, in a local Pennsylvania production, had been one of the most frustrating experiences of my life. Night after night I saw something happen in the theater that I had never seen before—an audience no longer made up of strangers, but friends, singing and rejoicing together. But although I felt their exhilaration, I was unable to share it—the Gospel narratives that the play is built around just didn't come alive for me.

Because acting was my whole world, I was willing to do anything to be a better actress—even if it meant going to the Bible to research my role. For the first time I really read the Gospels carefully. Now, waiting in the Ansonia Theater, I thought I was thoroughly prepared for the scene we were about to rehearse.

The director, an enthusiastic man, gave us our directions: "Jesus has just been arrested. You run to the spot where He was taken away. You look everywhere for Him, unable to believe what has happened. It's as though all your dreams have been shattered—everything you've loved and hoped for is gone."

As I began to play the scene, I felt a tremendous sadness rise and clutch my throat. Deeply moved, I burst into tears and allowed them to pour down my face. Everyone thought I was only acting. Afterward another member of the cast came up to me and said, "Claudia, that was great! How did you do it?"

"I don't know," I told her. And I really didn't. It didn't occur to me that I was acting out my own deep feelings of loss, fear, and loneliness, that the scene in the play was actually a scene from my life.

When the run of the play was over, I returned home to a routine that seemed even emptier and more aimless than before. I spent most nights in front of the television set wondering why my life had so little meaning.

One cold night in January, restless and unhappy, I opened the Bible. I came upon Revelation 3:20: "Behold, I stand at the door, and knock: if any man hear my voice, and open the door, I will come in to him, and will sup with him, and he with me." I began to think that Christ had been knocking at the door for a long time, at least since that long-ago night with Hal. Only Christ could know how to reach me through my desire to be a good actress, a desire that led me to the Bible and finally to Him. Suddenly an overwhelming surge of love and longing and gratitude flooded through me. Once again I went to my knees, this time thankfully welcoming my Savior into my life. At last I knew that my life was complete, and that I was made whole.

About a year after playing in *Superstar* I saw Hal again at another family get-together. Over coffee, I told him about all the changes that had entered into my life along with Christ. "For the first time I really feel I know what's important. It's not as if everything has been all roses, but when something disappointing happens—say I'm rejected for a part—I always have somewhere to turn. I'm never completely alone any more."

Hal was silent for a while. Then he said, "Well, I'm not surprised. I knew you were put in those two plays for a reason."

We ended that evening with thanksgiving for God's hidden guidance, for each other, and for the role that moved from the stage into my real life: disciple of Christ.

Faith Trusts God's Love and Care

Day of Faith

Elizabeth Neal Wells

However long and dark the night,
Day is sure to break
And children rise to laughter,
And birds to rapture wake.

However long the winter,
Spring will surely come,
Bringing gold of jonquil,
Silver of flowering plum.

However deep the sorrow,
However great the pain,
Be sure that peace will follow,
As sunlight follows rain.

My Friend Guideposts

Elaine St. Johns

Forty years ago *Guideposts* changed my life. And it came about in one of His mysterious ways.

At the age of thirty I found myself with two children, no visible means of support, and back home living with my mother. Nor had the genteel education for most young ladies of my day prepared me to earn a living.

Because he was a close friend, the publisher of a metropolitan tabloid, *The Los Angeles Mirror,* offered me a three-month trial job, a chance to "earn while you learn." Then, instead of placing me in the society or women's sections, which my age and background would indicate, he had me assigned city-side as a lowly cub reporter. In those three months, under constant pressure from deadlines, I learned a lot about writing fast and accurately. Which was good. But I also learned a lot of things I really didn't want to know.

For instance: the difference between a "leaper," a suicide who jumped from a window, and a "leaner," one who accidentally fell. About the seamier side of my native City of the Angels when I was invited to a bonfire meeting by a juvenile gang who wanted me truthfully to report conditions in their neighborhood (which I did). Up at the district attorney's office I learned why—way back then!—case after case of reported child molestation never came to trial. Families would not press charges because of fear of reprisal and the psychological effect on family and child from public exposure. We couldn't use the story, but I didn't sleep the night after reading those reports.

After a year of this shock treatment I had worked my way up to a very good salary and my own byline as a "sob sister," which meant I was sent on all the most tragic stories because pieces "by Elaine St. Johns" made readers cry. The reason they did was because I myself was crying inside most of the time. Crying and praying.

I didn't like what I was doing one little bit. I tried freelance writing, but the pieces I sent kept coming back. I tried to find another job, and couldn't. So I prayed for the sad, sorry world passing in review before me—and for guidance.

I remember covering the death of a little girl who fell into an abandoned sump hole. Amid frantic rescue efforts she talked bravely up to us for a time, then her voice was stilled forever. I wrote my story in a flood of tears, went home, threw myself on my knees, my faith at a low ebb.

"God," I cried, "I am trying to follow Your will for me, but I just can't believe this is it. To many, newspaper work would be exciting, but when I so want to write for Your glory, is this where You want me?" Then I whispered "Thy will be done," hoping I meant it, and the next day took my wavering faith back to the paper, where the days dragged on.

It was on a Saturday when I was home with my children that the accident occurred upon which my changed life was to pivot. My five-year-old daughter, Kristen, cut her hand by falling on some broken glass. I hurried her to the emergency room of a hospital. When we returned I found myself on my knees again, weeping now the cleansing tears of gratitude. For I had been the awed witness to the firm faith of a child.

I felt the urgent need to write about the experience, and more than that, I felt that somehow something was being asked of me. I wasn't sure what, but right then, with my daughter asleep in the next room, I sat down at the typewriter and this is what I wrote:

MY FRIEND GOD   Elaine St. Johns

My daughter, Kristen, has just turned six years old . . . a thoroughly joyous being who inhabits a small tanned body and inspects the world curiously through unperturbed blue eyes.

During her day of play it is very hard to tell when she is my daughter and when she is somebody else—Brave Heart, Gretel, or Hoppy.

Every so often, because of her high regard for the truth, and to keep the record straight between us, she reassures me.

"It's only a 'pretend,' Mommy," she confides to me suddenly. "I'm really your little girl, Kristen."

But she has one special friend with whom no liberties are taken. That is "my Friend God."

She introduced Him into our daily living when she was five. Sitting on the living room floor in a pool of sunbeams, Kristie seemed absorbed in crayoning. It should have been a quiet Sunday afternoon. But the radio had been nudged higher and higher so her uncle could hear the ball game above the noises that her brother, Koko, and I were making.

Suddenly over the din Kristie's voice rose.

"My Friend God wants me to have peace," she pleaded.

In the abashed silence that followed, Kristie didn't even look up. She continued her artwork.

Since then, I, who introduced them, have been humble before their ripening friendship. Humble, too, before the unfailing simplicity with which she approaches Him.

Where did she get her facts? She got them from the usual sources . . . Bible stories we read at home, Psalms we say together, from the little Sunday school where she and her playmates learn hymns. But the interpretation is strictly her own.

She has found that her Heavenly Father is always around, a thing she cannot truthfully say of her earthly parents. She is sure He created all things good and beautiful, hence He is a powerful ally, fully capable of assisting her with any problem. He has never let her down.

Take the matter of her red wagon. Did we, or did we not, lose it? One day it is there in its usual place, the next day it is gone.

We search diligently in all the possible places on our four acres. We ask Koko. We ask Grandma. We have done our best but we do not find it.

"Well," advises Kristie matter-of-factly, "we'd better ask God."

And because her blue eyes are fastened trustfully on mine, I sit down on the stone wall beside her and we ask. But I'm afraid it won't work.

Suddenly we are prompted to look in the coal shed, an unheard-of place for the red wagon anytime—especially during summer months.

We go to look. It is there. We hug each other, rejoicing.

Scrambling into the wagon and pushing off with one foot, Kristie says, "Thanks, God."

Or take the afternoon our terrace is inexplicably littered with broken flower pots where our hanging garden had come tumbling down.

"Kristen," says Grandma very kindly, "did you accidentally knock down those pots while playing?"

"No, Grandma." Her tight little braids shake emphatically.

"Kristie, are you sure?"

"I didn't break them, Grandma." She wants very much to be believed. "Ask God."

Two hours later we catch the neighbor's cat whisking the rest of them off with a playful paw.

Her Friend seems to have taught her a simple, infallible rule for brotherly love. Some of Kristie's playmates have noticed that her nurse-companion, Rose, is a Negro girl and have pointed out gleefully that her jovial friend from the telephone company is a "fat Mexican."

"Are Negroes and Mexicans close to God, Mother?" she asks.

That's how she sizes them up. People are either "close to God," like George Washington who never told a lie, or Hopalong Cassidy who used his smoking guns to save a widow's ranch . . . or they are people who "don't know about God yet," like cattle rustlers or a man she saw on the street who was quite drunk.

She has good-natured tolerance for those of us who "get away" from God temporarily by losing such human things as tempers or self-control. For there are times when she herself is not on the very best of terms with her Friend.

"Some days," she explains thoughtfully, "I just want to do what I want to do. I don't want to listen to Him."

These are very unpleasant days, crammed with tears and punishments, and I am always grateful when she has had enough and creeps quietly into her room to "get close" to Him again. I do not know if she talks to Him, or listens to Him, or prays. These matters are between her and her Friend.

On the adult plane where we scientific parents dwell, all this could be charming fancy well-laced with coincidence—except for one fact. Like the mountain climber who does not know the quality of the rope until he has fallen, so with my daughter's faith in her Friend. For she fell off the side of a mountain, and her rope held. Actually though, it was a small mountain.

But she had her bad spill while carrying a small glass bottle. A razor-sharp fragment from the broken glass cut deeply into the palm of her hand. When I reached her side, the blood was gushing upward in a terrifying, irregular fountain. I used my fingers as a tourniquet and soon she lay quietly in my lap while we contacted the emergency ward.

"I want to make a prayer," she told Grandma in a small voice. "But I haven't any words. You make the words, Grandma." But because Grandma's words were slow in coming, traveling as they must around a big grown-up lump of emotion, and because her need was urgent, Kristie patiently made her own prayer.

"God," she said, "You are my life. You love me. Even if all the blood runs out, You are my life. Even if I went in the den of lions with Daniel, You are my life. And," she sighed, "I love You."

In that confidence she rested.

At the hospital, the cool young doctor refused to perform the necessary surgery while I was in the room. My daughter lay there, very small in her bloody jeans, with her four freckles standing out on her little pug nose. I could not bear leaving her to face the ordeal alone.

"You just wait in the hall like the doctor says, Mommy," she advised.

For forty minutes I stood in that hallway and took strength from my small daughter's voice.

Once she yelped. Immediately she encouraged the doctor. "It's all right. I understand." But mostly she chatted with him about the everyday things in her life. How joyous she made it all sound . . . the triumph that my brother had "tooken my picture in Technicolor," the wonderful possibility of summer camp. Then she confessed a cherished secret.

She was not going to marry Hopalong Cassidy. She had seen a picture of Mrs. Hoppy in a magazine. Instead she was going to marry the tall Indian currently appearing in a color ad for a national railroad.

"Indians," I heard her inform the doctor, "are very close to God."

As I reentered the surgery, the young doctor put his arm on her shoulder. "Everything in her hand was laid wide open," he said gravely. "But your daughter has full use of all her fingers. No permanent damage. It was a miracle."

"It wasn't a miracle," said my little Indian firmly.

"It was my Friend God."

As the words flowed effortlessly onto the paper—and they did—I became aware of the quality of Kristen's faith. In my own relationship with her Friend I had complained, argued, rebelled. Kristen had simply trusted. "Except ye be converted, and become as little children," it says in Matthew (18:3). I was to need this conversion, for when I had finished Kristen's story, so joyously written, I knew that I should try to have it published. But more than that, I was now certain that no matter how much I needed the money, and I did, I would not sell the story. I made a vow that the article would be my tithe.

I sent it to my mother's agent in New York and it was accepted immediately by a prestigious national magazine with an enormous circulation. The magazine always paid top dollar, but it had no precedent for accepting gift material. "No national magazine will just take it for free," said our canny agent. "I thought you were kidding."

Then came the temptations. "Think of the exposure in that magazine," she said. "You can share with millions and give the money away." But my vow had been to give the article away. Logic or loyalty? Compromise or trust? Those ever-present questions for all trying Christians. Well, I wanted to be as loyal to Kristie's Friend as she had been, so—I trusted.

Finally our agent said, without much enthusiasm, "Your old friend Grace Perkins Oursler is now executive editor of a new inspirational magazine, a tiny periodical with a tiny circulation. She might take it." The name of the magazine? "Guideposts."

Grace took my tithing. And that article in Guideposts was the open sesame to my dream of inspirational writing. *Guideposts* took other pieces, assigned a few. Again I trusted. I quit my assured job on the paper to devote full time to writing on my own. There were other magazine articles. Books. Best of all I became a *Guideposts* Contributing Editor, then the West Coast Editor. Over a span of forty uninterrupted years my relationship with *Guideposts* has enriched my life in every way, including the ability to tithe financially far beyond the original *money* I was offered.

As for *exposure*. The little article about Kristen that had, as we say, "written itself" reached not only *Guideposts* subscribers but was read from pulpits by ministers, read over the air by one of the most popular news commentators of that day, Fulton Lewis, Jr. And five years after it appeared in print a fine New York artist, Dorothy Teichman, sent to me unsolicited three dozen charming illustrations inspired by Kris's story. These we incorporated into a children's book that was in print for many years. Apparently of its own volition the story was "shared with millions."

And what of those difficult days on the *Mirror?* Looking back I have to see that His will was best all down the line. In no other way, at my age, from a standing start, could I have learned the writing trade so quickly and thoroughly. In no other way could the protective shell of my self-centeredness have been shattered so quickly and thoroughly, giving my heart genuine compassion and the deep desire to serve the *Guideposts* ideal, "A Practical Guide to Successful Living," with true dedication.

I was sorely tempted to say, at the beginning of this tale, that *Guideposts* was my miracle, since it did indeed turn my life around. But now I can't. I must stand with Kristen.

The miracle was—and is—my Friend God.

The Lady Who Takes in Children

Sally Olsen

She was so tiny, so dirty, so very thin—and whenever I sat in the church she would come and snuggle against me. I couldn't understand the flow of words, not knowing any Spanish, except one that's clear in any language—*"mami."*

It got to be embarrassing—every evening this ragged little thing with her bare feet and matted hair clung to me like flypaper. I would slip into a pew at the rear; she would find me. I'd sit at the side; in seconds she'd be there.

Finally I spoke about it to the pastor who was interpreting for me during this visit to Puerto Rico. "That little girl sits beside me every evening and talks about her mother."

He gazed at me strangely. "She has no mother," he said. Carmencita, he explained, was an orphan whom members of the congregation were feeding. But all of them had large families of their own; none could afford an extra burden.

"She's asking *you* to be her mother."

Me! An unmarried forty-year-old missionary here from New York on a speaking trip? "I don't even know where *I'm* going to sleep tonight," I reminded him. Missionaries traveled on faith, accepting food and lodging from congregations where we spoke, traveling as God provided the means. And provide for me He had, through the warm and generous Puerto Ricans. But the whole idea of taking on a child was ridiculous.

Yet night after night, as the meetings in this particular church continued, Carmencita was there, seeking me out, curling up in the pew beside me.

And as I looked down at her, my mind went back to my own childhood in faraway Norway. Our family had been poor, although my father's job as a ship's mechanic kept bread on the table.

But when I was five years old, Father died. There were no jobs for women in our little fishing village and so Mother left the three younger girls with different families and went to Oslo with my older sister to search for work.

How crushing is the sense of being unwanted! One of my jobs for the family I stayed with was to drive their goats each morning to the square where the village goatherd collected the flocks for the daily trip to the mountain pasture. And in the square each morning, bringing her own goats, I saw a certain lady, and each day I wished I could go home with her.

I was seven years old when I finally got up courage to say so. "Would you like a girl? I can wash dishes and sweep and . . ."

She stooped down and put her arms around me. "All my life I've wanted a little girl. I would be so happy to have you live with me!" And so I did, for many happy years, until my own mother was able to bring her family together and take us all to America.

Now I had my plane reservation back to New York. The day before the flight I bought a little dress and a pair of shoes. The pastor handled the legal arrangements. Carmencita was beautiful as we entered the church together that night for a simple ceremony of adoption.

Back home in New York I put off explanations as long as I could. On the second day my mother came into my bedroom and closed the door.

"Sally," she said, speaking Norwegian as she always did when she meant business, "are you intending to keep this child?" When I nodded, she exploded with all the arguments I had given myself.

"Mother," I said, "let me tell you a true story." I had never mentioned to her my unhappiness in my first foster home, knowing that she had heartbreak enough of her own. Now I did, and I also told her about God's answer that I had seen in the face of a stranger. When I had finished she was silent for a while. Then she stood up.

"I'm going to make a cake. We're having a party."

And so we did—the next day—with my sisters and their husbands and children, as Carmencita was welcomed into the family.

And all the while I had the strangest feeling, as I was surrounded by my relatives, that God was telling me to go back to Puerto Rico. What possible work He could have for me there, a middle-aged woman who didn't even speak the language, I could not imagine. I took from the bank the money I had saved working as a maid and a file clerk, and Carmencita and I went back.

I started speaking again in the churches and, with Carmencita's help, learning Spanish. Then one day there was a knock at the door of the modest house we were renting. A very old, sickly woman stood there with four little boys who might have been grandchildren or great-grandchildren.

"Is this the place," she asked, "where children can come?"

I opened my mouth to ask what she meant, but to my astonishment, I answered, "Yes."

The place where children can come. Until I said it, I had not known it. They came from everywhere, from courts and government agencies, from relatives who could not keep them. Sometimes they were simply there when I opened the door in the morning.

When my family outgrew the first house, I rented the one next door too, and then the one next to that. The money came from every corner of Puerto Rico, occasionally a big gift, more often a single dollar bill in a much-handled envelope—for Puerto Ricans of every income level have a tremendous love for all children.

At first I would send the measurements of each child to New

York where my mother and sisters were kept busy over their sewing machines. But as word of our household got around, local women began sewing, cleaning, bringing food.

And still the children came. *I'm only one person,* I would think, *how can I do it all?* And then I remembered something my mother said when I was very small. "When we do what we can," she told me, "God does what He can."

The children were saving their pennies at that time to buy a horse. I knew the animal they had in mind—a sway-backed old nag living in a field down the street, lame, and, I suspected, half-blind, but beautiful to them. They worked hard all that summer, doing chores for the neighbors, bringing the piggy bank to me over and over, asking me to tabulate their savings.

Then one night, on the television set a friend had given us, we watched an Oral Roberts broadcast. He told of the need for Bibles in Israel, then asked for money. It grew very silent in our living room. Then: "What's an old horse?"

"Yeah! Who needs a horse!"

Carmencita ran for the piggy bank, and twenty-two little faces grew solemn as she cracked it open. It held $6.43; every penny went to Israel.

It was several days later that, against all my careful planning, I was caught in downtown San Juan at lunchtime—I always begrudged the money for restaurant meals. As I sat down I overheard three young men at the table next to mine speaking Norwegian and I simply couldn't resist joining the conversation.

They were on their way back to Scandinavia, they told me, after finishing an engineering project. "And by the way," one of them added, "we have a horse we don't know what to do with. You don't by any chance know of anyone who . . ."

And of course God's horse was beautiful, strong and straight and gentle, and the joy of the children for many years.

What God can do—every week, every day; every small human effort outmatched and outshone by His great supply. And not only our material needs but our spiritual and emotional ones as well.

Over five hundred children have called me *"mami"* now. Some are in college. Some are married with homes of their own.

Carmencita and her husband now have a child. And they keep coming—small, frightened, needing so much. *One woman,* I often think, *past sixty now [in 1973], and still so much need . . .*

And then I remember. I can do what I can—and my God will do the rest!

Prayer for Tomorrow

Carlene A. Wallace

Beyond today will be tomorrow,
But what it will bring of joy or sorrow
I cannot know. I only pray
Your guidance, Lord, each hour, each day
Your strength to bear whatever may be
Your loving wisdom has for me.
So sweet or bitter, sad or gay,
Be with me, Lord, beyond today.

The Blown-Away Hat

Louise Smith

In June of 1950, a house was lent to us on Galveston Bay so our two daughters and I could be with my husband while he worked in Houston. He was an engineering consultant dealing with the aftermath of explosions that had wrecked Texas City, Texas, three years earlier.

Charles drove to Houston every morning, returning about five o'clock. Lyn, five, Christie, three, and I spent lazy days fishing and playing in the water and on the sand.

I'd bought new straw hats for the children to shade them from the fierce Gulf Coast sun. One day, about mid-morning, when a brisk breeze was blowing, we went to do "worm-fishing" from the end of the pier in front of the cabin. Lyn's hat blew into the water.

"Please get it, Mother," she begged. "It's so close, see? And it's brand new!"

Wavelets rocked the hat gently away from the pier. I eyed the rowboat tied beneath the pier. It was kept there for rowing out to the buoy where the speedboat was hitched. The hat was hardly a boat's length away. But I was wary because, as a native of Central Texas, I was unfamiliar with the waves and currents in the bay; I knew only gentle lakes.

"Let it go," I told Lyn. "These waves might be strong enough to be dangerous. We can get you another hat."

"Please, Mother! I won't let it blow off again. I'll hold it on."

I looked around. On the next pier, not a hundred yards away, a man sat fishing, his straw hat pulled low. I thought he might be asleep, but at least if I had a problem, there was an adult who could get help. I warned the girls against falling into the water, went down the ladder into the boat, untied the rope, and pushed off.

It didn't take me long to know I was in trouble. The hat, an oar's length away, floated soggily and slowly. The boat moved farther out to sea with each wave. I decided to forget the hat and get back to where I belonged.

I put my back into it, but with each stroke, the boat was farther out. *I could not get back!*

I called to the neighboring fisherman, but he did not respond.

"Lyn," I called, "take Christie's hand and walk off the pier, to the shore. Then go and wake that man on the next pier. Show him I'm out here. Ask him to help me." Lyn began to cry.

"Don't be afraid," I told her, "he'll know what to do. I'm all right." She ran, forgetting I'd told her to walk, but soon she was beside the fisherman. By then I was so far away it was hard to understand what she was saying when she called to me.

"It's not a man," she screamed. "It's not real!"

I was stunned. It was someone's idea of a joke to put a pole in the hand of a dummy, bait can beside it, at the pier's end.

I cupped my hand around my mouth and yelled. "Go back and stop at the houses along the shore road. Knock and yell until someone comes. If you can't find anyone at the first house, or the next one, keep trying."

It was all I could do. Lyn gave me a nod and a wave and took off along the pier, dragging Christie by the hand.

As I drifted farther away, I could see her at the first house, then at the second. The children were stumbling down the dusty lane toward a distant third. Then a new realization hit me: the houses were empty! They belonged to people who worked in the city and came to the bay in the evenings or on weekends.

I thought of trying to swim back, but if I could not row against the current, how could I hope to swim against it?

I knew I was in the ships' channel, which could take me past Galveston Island into the Gulf of Mexico. If the children could not find help, I might be run down by a big ship, or drift into the Gulf to die of thirst. Abruptly I cut off that kind of thinking. I had always fought against picturing bad things that could happen.

Locked out of the cottage, alone and without water as the day wore on into blazing afternoon heat, the children would wander around frightened in a strange place. *Who,* or *what,* might answer their knock? Once again I shut my mind against those ugly pictures.

I had to stop thinking; but I had to fill my mind with something. It seemed too obvious to pray, if what is meant by prayer is crying, "Help me, God." No, I would not pray. I knew God was there. He knew I was there, and He knew better than I what kind of help I needed. I didn't pray to Him to stop the wind, to reverse the drift, or to let the children find someone who would call the Coast Guard.

Prayer is being with *Him,* I thought. So I determined to be as close to Him as possible. I thought about how good He had been to me all my life. I thought about how, for most of my years, I had been astonished at His goodness, never quite able to believe it, wondering why He took such care of me. Even though I'd been through some rough times, it seemed to me that He'd always carried the heavier end of the load, that He'd always shown me that life could be good once we got over a particularly nasty patch, and that, most of all, it was *all right,* whatever happened to me.

God simply was not going to stop looking after me on that hot June day in Galveston Bay. If I could keep the feeling that it would be all right whatever happened to me, then it *would* be all right. What I needed was the strength to trust Him absolutely.

I pulled my hat to shade as much of me as it would, and then I waited . . .

In Houston, Charles was listening to a complex problem about liability relating to a plant destroyed in the fire following the explosions of the ships *Grand Camp* and *High Flyer* at the Texas City docks in 1947. Suddenly he got up.

"I'm sorry," he told the lawyers and other engineers, "I have to leave." He had no idea why. He didn't even wonder why. He just knew he had to get back to our house on the Bay.

Charles drove as fast as he could. In less than forty-five minutes he arrived. On the way to our lane he saw Lyn and Christie. They were hot, dirty, and smeared with tears, but they were still going faithfully from door to door along the shore.

As I drifted ever farther out in the Bay, I kept my eyes on the cottage. I saw a blue speck moving on shore. I wondered if it could be our car. I waved my hat, but I doubted that anyone could see even the boat since it dipped and rose on waves that had grown bigger as I drifted farther from shore.

Soon, so soon that I could hardly believe it, Charles roared across the water in the speedboat. I was rescued.

We did not fling ourselves into each other's arms. He helped me cross from the rowboat to the cruiser, tied on the boat, and back we went, not trying to explain over the sounds of the wind and the motor.

I felt too exalted to talk—and so did Charles—not just because I was safe, but because both of us, in our separate situations, had managed to trust God. And the most thrilling thing of all was that God had allowed us to trust Him. He let both of us, at the same time, rely on Him without question.

At last we were back at the buoy and finally at the pier and into the house. I held two sun-scalded little bodies to me and felt my husband's grasp. *Then* I prayed—in thankfulness.

Get Out Before It Blows!

Franklin Brandt

It was one of those days that makes being a trucker something special. The weather was cool for July; the morning was bright. I had eaten a good breakfast and was feeling great as I rolled down the Ohio Turnpike just out of Cleveland. There was a curve in the road up ahead. As I started into it, a station wagon filled with kids moved past me. The kids waved and I waved back.

Suddenly the steering wheel went loose under my hands. I spun it in one direction, then back again—but my rig just kept moving straight ahead, off the highway. I could see the crash coming. My rig, loaded with a dangerous cargo of flammable chemicals, bounced off the road toward a shallow gully. For a fraction of a second I flew through the air. The front wheel hit the far side of the gully. Then the drive axle hit too and I knew we were going over. The tractor, with me bouncing around inside, turned upside down and landed wheels-over-roof at the edge of the highway.

As the dust cleared, I tried to move. Nothing. I was lying on my chest and stomach, pressed against the upside-down roof of the tractor, my face just a few inches off the ground. The engine must have wrenched loose; boiling oil dripped down my legs.

But the real danger was in that cargo. Behind me in the trailer were dozens of steel drums filled with industrial chemicals. They were safe unless they got themselves mixed together. Then they would start to "work." They would grow hotter and hotter until finally they'd explode. How long would that take? An hour? Two hours? "Well, Lord," I said aloud, "I'm in Your hands whether I live or die."

I felt someone tap me on my shoulder. I lifted my head and could just make out through the shattered window the form of a young man.

"I'm the guy with the kids, from the wagon," he said. "My wife's gone for help. Can I do anything?"

"Where's the trailer?"

"On its back behind you. It's smoking."

"Yeah. See if you can get that door open, will you? And then get out of here. You don't want to be around if that thing blows."

The guy tugged and pulled but it was useless. "I'll stay here and talk to you," he said. Fumes from the trailer began to blow up against us. The guy started coughing. I couldn't get him to leave. Soon there were other people too, truckers mostly, living up to our code of sticking by each other. One old geezer stuck his head in the window.

"We've sent for a wrecking crew," he said. He told me he had been trucking most of his life and he'd got men out of wrecks before. "What are you carrying?"

"Sodium hydrosulfite. It'll blow if it gets too hot."

I must have passed out then. The next thing I knew there was a whirring in my ears and I felt a breeze from a saw that was cutting through the metal cab. The guy with the saw wore a mask and the other men huddled near him had handkerchiefs over their faces against the fumes.

"How long's he been in there?" one of the firemen was asking. His voice was high-pitched and anxious, and he kept looking back over his shoulder toward the trailer.

"An hour."

The guy was a lot more excited than I was, and as I began to talk to him and the others, my calmness seemed to help them. I knew where it came from too. All the time I was lying pinned in the tractor I was praying. I heard the fireman say, "He sure is cool." He seemed to want to talk. Who'd I work for? I was an independent. Where was I from? Minnesota. Any family? Yeah, a wife and two kids. The fireman asked me if the cargo was dangerous.

"It's dangerous, all right. If you're smart, you'll get out of here."

The old trucker heard me and laughed. "We'll go—when we get you out," he said. He seemed to know just what to do. He told the three wrecking crews exactly how to hook up. They obeyed. "Easy now, easy. Back up a bit. Now let's lift her." I could feel the engine lift an inch. Half a dozen hands reached through the hole in the side of my cab and tried to pull me out. It was no good; my legs were still pinned by the crushed cab.

"We'll try one more time," said the old man. "Just one more time."

I passed out again. Then I heard a state trooper trying to clear the area. Those chemicals had been working for two hours, he said. You could feel the heat.

"Come on," said the trooper to the old trucker. "You too."

But he was busy hooking up the wreckers again. "One more time," he said. "Just once more." They did what he said while the fireman and the trooper sweated and I kept up my silent conversation with the Lord. "Easy now," said the old man. "Easy." I heard the low grinding whir of the winches and again I could feel the weight lifting off my back.

"Come on," said the fireman. "That trailer's really smoking."

"Just another inch," said the old-timer. "That's it . . . now," he said through the hole in the side of the cab, "we're going to pull. Let's go."

Strong hands grabbed my head, shoulders, clothing. They pulled, and I wiggled and pushed as best I could.

And suddenly I began to move. An inch at a time, one foot at a time. While the smoke grew thicker around us, I was jerked out of my cab until at last I lay on the ground inside a circle of truckers, police, firemen, and workmen. I tried to thank them but everyone was in a hurry to get out of there. I couldn't stand up. They put a stretcher next to me and rolled me onto it. I am a heavy man. It took six men to carry me across the washout.

The last thing I remember was hearing the door of the ambulance close. But the next day the state trooper was beside me in the hospital. He had brought me the Bible I had carried beside me in the cab and which somehow had not been hurt. He told me that the minute the ambulance started for the hospital the trailer exploded. One of the five hundred-pound drums was thrown three hundred feet. More than $45,000 worth of gear was reduced to scrap in one second.

"You got insurance?"

"I do."

"You know, mister, I think you got another kind of insurance too. I saw that sign on your truck. You know the one?" Yes, I knew. "I guess that's how come you could stay so calm," said the trooper.

That's how come, all right. That sign the trooper was talking about, it says everything: "Christ is my rock and my salvation."

Faith Believes
God's Promises

&

Perennial

Norma Weathersby Blank

The world is full of miracles
And not the least of these
Are bulbs I plant in autumn
Beneath the drifting leaves.

I feel a strange excitement
As I place them in the sod—
Committing them, in dark and cold,
To do the will of God.

The sunny days grow shorter now
November's breath is chill
My faith by definition is—
Bulb equals daffodil!

The Seekers

Edith Dean

Out on the porch I leaned against a splintery column. I was five years old and I was waiting for Mom to come back from "mailbox hill." On days as hot as this, you could see the heat devil-dancing across our seared vegetable garden and the parched cornfield beyond.

Mom came into view across the fields. Even at a distance her trudging gait told me there was no letter from Dad. He was away from home and sent money when he could find work. We needed that money for food.

Mom's shoulders lifted resolutely as she approached the gate. I knew how disappointed she was. I knew too that she was just as hungry as I was, yet her faith in God did not waver. She patted my head, saying "God has always taken care of us, Edith. He will now. Jesus said, 'Ask, and it shall be given you, seek, and ye shall find' " (Matthew 7:7).

Removing her battered straw hat, she started into the house. Suddenly she put her hat back on, turned toward me, and repeated, "Seek, and ye shall find," as though God had rewarded her faith with instructions. "Tell you what," she said. "Let's go fishing. We'll cook our catch beside Mallow's pond." She tried to make it sound like a picnic, but it didn't quite come off. For I remembered the picnics we'd had just for fun when it wasn't so important whether or not we caught a fish.

I took the black skillet off the nail inside the cupboard door. Mom rummaged around in the attic for some old fishing stuff that "will have to do," took the box of matches from its holder beside the stove and a knife from the rack above the warming shelf.

Mom didn't even scold me when I let the screen door slam behind me. Maybe, just this once, the loud, bold sound made *her* feel better too. But she did send me back for my straw hat. And while I was inside I picked up my picture book of Bible stories.

We trudged through dead-silent woods. All the small woodland inhabitants were quiet; they had found the coolest spot they could to wait out the burning heat of the day. As we followed the narrow path, bushes snapped stingingly across our legs. Even in the shade the earth was hot to my bare feet; in the sun it seemed to scorch them.

As I lagged behind, Mom went ahead to cut a sapling pole and to dig a few worms near the almost-dry spring. I seemed to know that if for just a moment she gave in to her weariness she might lose her determination to "seek."

At last we stood beside the blue-green pond. It threw our reflections back at us, neither welcoming nor rejecting. It was cooler here, but I was hungrier than ever.

I watched Mom bait her hook, stand up, and throw the line as far as she could toward the middle of the pond. Then she sat on a log that had been uprooted during a windstorm, a study in determination. But the fish were not biting.

As the long afternoon wore on, I turned listlessly through the pages of my Bible stories. Now and then I slept fitfully. Each time I awoke, I hoped Mom had caught at least one little fish. Each time I was disappointed.

The woods began to come alive. The rustle amid the dry leaves told us that crawling and burrowing animals had come out for the evening. The shadows of the water bugs skittering across the surface of the pond were almost three feet long before Mom finally gave up. "God must have another answer for us," she said in quiet acceptance.

I felt too weak to walk home. I looked accusingly at the pond. For one brief moment, on the far edge of the water, the late afternoon sun turned a golden spotlight on perch swimming near the surface.

"Mom," I called, running to her side, "maybe it's like the men that fished all night. They didn't catch nothin' either. An' Jesus told 'em to try the other side. 'Member?" I pointed to a picture in my book: "Look!" Huge nets overflowed with fish; the sturdy fishing boat listed dangerously (John 21:2–6).

Mom stopped and glanced at the picture. Then she turned toward the dim path that wound around the old pond.

In my newly found enthusiasm I followed at her heels. Even when you're five, there are some things you just know. And I knew Mom would catch fish.

"I'll pick up some branches for the fire," I volunteered. And Mom, adding to my act of faith, put the frying pan on some stones before she began to fish.

After we'd eaten, Mom decided it was cool enough to "salt one away" for our breakfast. While she cleaned it, she said, "Honey, there's a lesson in this for us. I'd forgotten what Jesus was telling those men about seeking and finding. He was saying, 'Don't get discouraged if things are not going right in one place. Try the other side.' "

To this day I still remember how good those fish tasted, and how they nourished both my body and my faith.

Standing on God's Promise
Benjamin S. Carson, M.D.

The mother and father standing before me in the consulting room would not believe there was no hope for their four-year-old son. They had brought him to Johns Hopkins from their home in Georgia, where he had been diagnosed as having a malignant tumor of the brain stem, that knoblike cluster on top of the spine through which all brain impulses flow. The little blond boy was paralyzed, comatose; his blue eyes gyrated sightlessly.

I suffered with the parents. I had three small sons of my own. Yet I had studied the X rays revealing the dark, ugly mass and discussed them with the radiologists and others on the staff. "I'm so very sorry, Mr. and Mrs. Pylant," I said, "but there is no way in which we can encourage you."

The mother's chin quivered. "That's what they told us in Georgia, doctor, but the Lord led us to bring Christopher to Baltimore because He made it plain there was a doctor here who could help him. We believe you are that doctor."

"But I . . ."

"It's not in the mind of the Lord to let our little boy die, doctor," broke in the father, nervously twisting the brim of his fedora. "Will you please operate?"

In the face of such faith what could one say?

"I'll do my best," was all I could reply.

The next morning after my regular Scripture reading, I prayed, asking God to guide my hands and mind in the complicated operation facing me. In communing with Him, I thought about all the unbelievable things He had wrought in my life since I was growing up in Detroit's inner city.

My mind drifted back to those days when my mother raised my

older brother, Curtis, and me all by herself. She worked hard at three jobs at once, housekeeping in other peoples' homes, caring for their children.

She prayed every day for Curtis and me, and on Saturdays took us with her to the Seventh-day Adventist Church. I loved the stories about the prophets and Jesus and His healings. And when I heard how the mission doctors helped people in far-off lands, I vowed right then and there to become a physician.

I told my mother about my dream as we walked home along the glass-strewn sidewalks one night. Aware of the hopeless-looking men standing in doorways and the squad car racing up the street, she stopped and put her hands on my shoulder. "Benny, if you ask the Lord for something, *believing* He will do it, then He *will* do it."

But my mother was also well aware of my poor marks in elementary school, and she proceeded to let me know it would also take a lot of work on my part.

"You will never become a doctor if all you do is watch television," she said one morning as she snapped off *The Three Stooges*. "You and your brother had better start reading something."

She insisted that we read at least two books a week. "Don't you touch that knob, Benny," she'd order if ever she caught me reaching for the TV. "Read your book."

And so I did, and the more I read, the more interesting books became. Before long I was devouring them.

Within two years I rose from the bottom of my class to the top. My good marks won honors in high school, which earned me a scholarship to Yale University, then the University of Michigan Medical School, and eventually helped me realize another long-held dream, a staff appointment at Johns Hopkins Hospital.

But how easily none of these things might have happened.

One of the problems I had as a kid was my violent temper. It was so severe that when it exploded I'd even attack others with a rock, brick, or anything else at hand. No matter how hard I tried to control it, my temper would snap like an old rattrap.

One day when I was fourteen, a boy in our neighborhood was tormenting me. Suddenly everything flashed red. Snatching a big camping knife, I lunged fiercely at his stomach.

Crack! The steel blade snapped as it struck his heavy metal belt-buckle.

As the boy fled in terror, something also snapped in me. I was shocked at what I had nearly done: I might have *killed* that boy. Sickened, I stumbled home where I shut the bathroom door and slumped on the porcelain tub, staring at the wall.

How could I help myself? I knew that my temper was out of control. Something had to be done.

At that time in church we'd been reading the Book of Proverbs. It was my favorite book—as it is now. As I sat on the edge of the tub, some of Solomon's words began to form slowly in my mind: *He that hath no rule over his own spirit . . .*

I couldn't help but feel that there was meaning for me in those words: *He that hath no rule over his own spirit is like a city that is broken down, and without walls* (25:28).

They *were* meant for me; I knew now for certain that I had to get control of my spirit. If I didn't I'd end up in jail, or dead.

"Ask the Lord, Benny, *believing* that He will . . ." Mother had said again and again.

Right then and there I knelt on the bathroom floor. "O Lord," I prayed, "take away my temper. I know, I *believe* You will."

And He did. There wasn't anything gradual about it at all. The Lord took away my temper, just like that. Whenever I'd feel it begin to boil, it would somehow simmer down as if someone had turned off the burner. I was in awe at what had happened to me, and I remained so.

When the time came to operate on little Christopher Pylant, I looked at my hand, the one that had wielded the knife that fateful day, and I gave thanks that it was about to guide what I hoped would be a lifesaving scalpel.

That morning in the operating room, after I'd opened the back of Christopher's little shaven head, it was just as I expected: malignant dark tumor everywhere. I couldn't even see the brain stem, which evidently had been consumed by the cancer. Without the brain stem, there is no real life.

We excised as much of the tumor as safely possible, closed the incision, and had the boy taken to the intensive-care unit.

As I stepped into the waiting area, the parents rose with expectant faces. I didn't have the heart to tell them there was no hope, but I had to.

"I'm sorry we couldn't help your son," I said. "I know you both have prayed and I have prayed too. But sometimes the Lord works in ways we don't fully understand."

The mother and father did not flinch. Both still maintained that earnest look of conviction.

"Doctor," the father said as his wife nodded in agreement, "the Lord is going to heal our son. We're standing on His promise."

Taking a deep breath, I could only add, "Your faith is admirable."

I felt so very sorry for the Pylants who believed so strongly in something so hopeless. What I had seen in Christopher's brain was irrefutable.

However, three days after the operation something strange happened. Though Christopher was still comatose, his eyes began focusing and his physical movements began improving.

"Let's repeat his CT scan," I said, a peculiar feeling going through me.

As I studied the scan printout, I was amazed to see a tiny threadlike remnant of brain stem.

We had to go back in.

The next day, Christopher was back in surgery and I was again working on that discolored malignant tissue with scalpel and forceps. But where it had seemed so impossible to define planes before, I was suddenly able to lift the mass away in layers. I became excited. A nurse wiped perspiration from my brow as I worked. At last, after cleaning out all the crevices, there it lay, the healthy gray brain stem, intact, but flattened and distorted.

Within a month our patient was ready to leave the hospital. With Christopher smiling up at us, his parents and I thanked the Lord together. As they walked out of the hospital, the glory shone on their faces, and I heard my mother telling me once again: *"If you ask the Lord for something believing He will do it, then He will do it."*

Editor's note: *Dr. Carson was the primary surgeon in the dramatic and successful twenty-two-hour operation in September 1987 separating the West German Siamese twins joined at the head. He has also performed a number of hemispherectomies, a rare and critical operation in which half of a child's brain is removed to keep him or her from deteriorating or dying of a rare seizure disorder, Rasmussen's encephalitis, which initially affects only one hemisphere of the brain. Those children have recovered almost all faculties, since the remaining half of the brain evidently takes on the functions of the other.*

Dr. Carson (whose middle name is Solomon) reads Proverbs "for wisdom" in the morning and at night.

He graduated magna cum laude from high school, attended Yale University and the University of Michigan School of Medicine, interned and took residency at Johns Hopkins, and was senior neurological registrar for one year at Sir Charles Gairdner Hospital, western Australia's major neurosurgery center. He returned to Johns Hopkins in 1984 and at age thirty-three was made its director of pediatric neurosurgery.

He Will Not Forsake My Children

Alice Hayes Taylor

We *thought* the children were safe, there on the coast of China—safe from anything. Until the Japanese invaders came.

James and I were Free Methodist missionaries, a husband-and-wife team, deep in the Chinese province of Henan.* Our four children were in the Chefoo School in Shandong Province, a thousand miles away. My husband had attended that school. His grandfather, James Hudson Taylor I, had *started* it. The school had known four generations of Taylors, and the teachers were more family than not.

My father-in-law, Herbert Taylor, was there in Chefoo,† too. I felt as if the children were in their own home, safe and snug. I was an American, my husband was British. We'd long been missionaries. So it seemed to me that the children would be safe anywhere in the world.

Then suddenly the Japanese swept into China. Mortars screamed overhead. Bombs plunged to the earth, maiming and killing people. Entrapping and scattering people. We were cut off! It was impossible to get back to Chefoo.

Pushing farther inland from the east, the Japanese overran Henan in 1939, and James and I ran for our lives. I was six months pregnant at the time. We escaped to the town of Fangxian, far, far inland, on the western border of Shaanxi. But my thoughts were constantly in Chefoo.

How could I have known when I married into the Taylor family, missionaries to the Chinese since the 1800s, that this was how life would turn out? I had melded into their ways: of teaching and loving and sharing with the Chinese, of riding bicycles or walking or hiring the jolting horse-drawn carts, of eating with chopsticks and sleeping on a mat atop a large brick bed. China was home, and when the war came, disrupting the lives of the Chinese, splitting apart families, it did the same to the Taylors.

I sent frequent letters to Chefoo, telling the children where we were and somehow, miraculously, a few letters came to us from the

---

*Spellings of Chinese names have been changed to conform to current practice in China.

†The town of Chefoo is now known as Yantai.

children. They'd had Sunday dinner with Grandpa. Kathleen, four-teen, had earned another Girl Guides badge. Jamie, ten, had breezed through his exams. Mary had just celebrated her ninth birthday. John, eight, had been sick, but was much better. And, briefly, there had been some ground skirmishes between Japanese troops and Chinese guerrillas, but the school had escaped harm, and the fighting subsided.

I would take out the children's letters and reread them until they became frayed at the edges. I agonized over the lack of news. "James," I would say, "do you think the children are all right? It's been so long since we've heard anything."

With his quiet faith, James reassured me. But I saw the worry in his eyes. And I knew that his very human fear for the children's safety was just as great as mine.

I pictured them over and over—the times we had spent to-gether reading and talking and singing around the organ. I remem-bered them the way they looked the day James and I left Chefoo—Kathleen in a navy blue jumper and white blouse, her long, wavy hair falling past her shoulders; Mary with her blonde bob and pretty blue eyes; our sons, so young and full of promise.

"Heavenly Father, keep them safe," I prayed. "Watch over Grandpa Taylor."

The air raids sent us running for shelter day after day. Epidem-ics and disease raged among the Chinese soldiers. In parts of China, food was so scarce because of drought that people were eating tree bark. In the midst of this, with missionaries helping with relief programs, passing out food and clothes to refugees, James and I started the Northwest Bible Institute to prepare young people for the ministry. Somehow, we knew, God's work had to go on; and we spent long hours developing a curriculum and preparing teach-ers, then enrolling students.

One day, after teaching a class, I was just entering our house when the newspaper deliveryman came. The paper's large Chinese characters announced: "Pearl Harbor Attacked. U.S. Enters War." As I absorbed the news, I realized why there had been a long silence from the children. *Chefoo had been in the Japanese line of attack.*

"O dear God," I whispered, "my children, my children . . ." I knelt beside the bed. Not even tears came at first, just wave after wave of anguish.

As the fear penetrated deeper, I remembered the horror stories of Nanjing—where all of the young women of that town had been brutally raped. And I thought of our lovely Kathleen, beginning to blossom into womanhood . . .

Great gulping sobs wrenched my whole body. I lay there, gripped by the stories we had heard from refugees—violent deaths, starvation, the conscription of young boys—*children*—to fight.

I thought of ten-year-old Jamie, so conscientious, so even-tempered. "What has happened to Jamie, Lord? Has someone put a gun in *his* hands? Ordered him to the front lines? To death?"

Mary and John, so small and so helpless, had always been inseparable. "Merciful God," I cried, "are they even alive?"

Kneeling there by the bed, pleading with God, I knew without any doubt at all that I had no other hope but God. I reached out to Him now, completely. "Please help my children. Let them be alive, *please!*" Then, as if in a dream, I drifted back to a time when I was a girl of sixteen in Wilkes-Barre, Pennsylvania. I pictured our minister, Pa Ferguson, sitting there telling me words he had spoken years ago: "Alice, if you take care of the things that are dear to God, He will take care of the things dear to you." That was Pa Ferguson's translation of "Seek ye first the kingdom of God, and his righteousness; and all these things shall be added unto you" (Matthew 6:33). It was his way of making his point to the teenagers he was working with.

In the stillness of the bedroom, I pondered Pa Ferguson's words. Who were the ones dear to God? The Chinese to whom God had called me to minister. And who were the ones dear to me? My children.

I did not know whether my children were dead or alive. Nevertheless a deep peace replaced my agony. This war had not changed God's promise. With that assurance, I felt the aching weight of fear in my stomach lift.

"All right, God," I said finally, "John and Mary and Kathleen and Jamie are in Your care. With all my heart I believe that You will guard them. I know that You will bring us back together, and until that day comes, I will put all my energy into Your work. *I promise.*"

We had a pact, God and I, and I knew He would keep His part of it. And I must keep mine.

So it went, each day—taking care of the things dear to God. Like the day at the house of Mr. Chang, whose body and mind were devastated by disease. "He will not let anyone near the house," his wife warned.

I walked to the window and called, "Mr. Chang, we have come to pray for you. You can be healed. Please let us come in." And he did! He turned his life over to God. *And I knew that God was watching over my children.*

There were times when I rode into the hills with our new baby, Bertie, strapped on my back and held open-air meetings with people in remote villages. "This is for You, Heavenly Father," I would say in prayer, "because these are Your children, dear to You." *And I knew that He was caring for my children, too.*

And in the compound, when I worked as a midwife delivering babies, I would say to God, "Thank You for letting me deliver this child." *And I thanked Him for delivering my children from harm.*

In time we received word that everyone in Chefoo School had been captured and crammed into a concentration camp in Weihsien (now known as Weifang) along with thirteen hundred other captives. But we had no way of knowing, from day to day, whether the children were alive.

People would say to me, "You have such great strength, Alice, carrying on, yet knowing that your children have been captured."

And I would say, "My strength is God's strength. I know He will not forsake my children. I know this."

Through it all—the scarcity, the sickness, the dying, through the bombings when I didn't breathe until I heard the explosion and realized I was still alive—I did what I knew God wanted me to do. I took care of the Chinese. I passed along His Word to doctors, to army officers and troops, to students, to parents and grandparents. Over and over. Day after day.

In spare moments after school I began sewing clothes for Kathleen and Mary.

"What is that you're making, wifey?" James asked, using his usual term of endearment.

"Some pajamas for the girls, James, for when they come back. I hope I've judged the sizes right."

He was silent. Just looked at me.

Then one Sunday morning, as I held services in a village twenty miles from Fangxian, one of the students from the Bible Institute appeared in the crowd, pushing my bicycle, and announced, "They say that the Japanese have surrendered!"

The crowd burst into excitement. But for days, confusion reigned. Families had been torn apart, homes demolished, records lost or burned. Communication and transportation were haphazard. People groped for life and roots.

I longed to hear some word, just to know . . . And as I sat one September evening in our home during a faculty meeting, my mind wandered once more to the children. Again I pictured them as I had seen them last, waving good-bye. I heard their voices, faintly, calling excitedly . . . then I heard their voices *louder*. Was I imagining this? No, their voices were real!

And they came bursting through the doorway. "Mommy, Daddy, we're home, we're home!" And they flew into our arms. Our hugs, our shouts filled the room. We couldn't let go of one another. It had been five and a half long, grueling years. Yet, there they were—thin, but alive and whole, laughing and crying. Oh, they had grown! But Kathleen still wore the same blue jumper she had worn when I last saw her. It was as though God had miraculously preserved the children and returned them to us.

Later, medical checkups showed their health to be excellent. There were no emotional repercussions, and when we went to the States a year later, our children were *two years* ahead of students their own age.

While many in Japanese concentration camps suffered horrors, the children of the Chefoo School were spared. They received dedicated care from their teachers, and when there was not enough food to go around, the teachers helped the children gather wild edible plants. They continued their lessons and they attended church. Jamie looked after Grandpa Taylor, who was flown back to England after the war. And today Jamie—James Hudson Taylor III—works with the Overseas Missionary Fellowship in Singapore.

For our family, that advice from Pa Ferguson long years ago will always hold special meaning. I pass it along to you, for it is truly so: "If you take care of the things that are dear to God, He will take care of the things dear to you."

Mary Remembers the Day . . .   *Mary Taylor Previte*

I will never forget that sight—large yellow and white poppies floating down from the sky. American paratroopers dropped to the ground, and like a great human sea, all fourteen hundred captives swept out of our concentration camp to meet them!

Grandpa Taylor was on the first planeload flown out; we four Taylor children were on the second. We were flown to Xian, a hundred miles from home. A Chinese friend of Father's took us by train to within fifteen miles of Fangxian, then hired a cart and began driving us in the rain down the rutted road. It was dusk.

But the mule was too slow for us, and we jumped off the cart and raced ahead, sloshing barefoot through the mud until we met one of our parents' students, who led us through a moon gate, then across the Bible school compound. We saw our parents through the window, and we ran stumbling and shouting, "Mommy! Daddy!" through the doorway and into their arms.

Years ago, Mother had taught us to sing Psalm 91: "He that dwelleth in the secret place of the most High shall abide under the shadow of the Almighty. . . ." God *had* been with us those five and a half years. And the night he brought us back together was like a dream come true. No, it was even more; it was a *promise* come true.

A Lesson in Trust

Brenda Cox

Never, I thought, *has December been bleaker.* I stood at the living room window, staring at the leafless trees, their limbs shivering in the cold wind that whooshed down the street. I had just put the children to bed—three-year-old Tiffani and two-month-old Chad, my beautiful new baby whose hospital delivery had totally wiped out what little savings we'd had. I heard my husband, Sam, clattering around in our bedroom—what he always did after one of our arguments.

Why had I snapped at him? I shut my eyes as though that would prevent the tears from flowing. I knew he was too proud to apply for food stamps—why must I always bring it up? I had never known such gnawing worry. Sam's last two paychecks had bounced, and daily, like so many nightmares, the checks we'd written against them kept returning in the mail. We'd learned that the company Sam worked for was slowly going out of business and the owner was under investigation for dishonest practices. Sam could not find work, and we were broke and in debt.

I turned away from the window and went to sit on the couch. On the end table was my white leather Bible, a wedding gift. I picked it up and ran my fingertips across its cover. Sam and I read and studied the Bible together some evenings. I heard Sam's footsteps coming down the hall. *Thank goodness*, I breathed. He sat next to me and took my hand.

"What are we going to do?" I said. He shrugged listlessly. Poor Sam. It was so important to him to be able to provide for us.

"We could always borrow," he said. I didn't answer. I didn't have to. We'd borrowed so heavily from our parents at the beginning of our marriage that neither of us wanted to ask again. "I guess not," he answered for me. "So what *do* we do?"

I opened the Bible to Matthew 6:31–33. "I've read these verses maybe twenty-five times today," I said, "but I just don't know whether I can believe it. It just sounds like so many words . . ."

"Well, try it again," Sam said.

"Therefore take no thought, saying, What shall we eat? or, What shall we drink? or, Wherewithal shall we be clothed? (For after all these things do the Gentiles seek:) for your heavenly Father knoweth that ye have need of all these things. But seek ye first the kingdom of God, and his righteousness; and all these things shall be added unto you."

As I read, a gentle stirring of hope and understanding awakened within me. I glanced at Sam, wondering if he felt it too. "That's Jesus Himself talking," Sam said. "We just can't ignore it."

"Seek ye first the kingdom of God," I whispered. "That's what we haven't been doing. Instead we've borrowed money whenever we could. Then, we've worried. We've sought the kingdom of God *last*, after trying to take care of everything else."

Sam sighed and squeezed my hand tight. "You're right. Well, this time maybe we'd better find out if Jesus meant what He said. But how do you seek the kingdom of God first?"

We both prayed silently for insight in the quiet moments that followed. Then Sam said, "I think the most important thing is to follow God's will in every situation, and to follow it no matter how hard it may be."

"Then we've got to trust Him absolutely," I said. "Perhaps we shouldn't ask for any financial help at all, or even tell anybody about our problems."

We continued talking for a long time. We worked out two basic rules in our "searching out" of the kingdom: (1) In every situation to seek and follow God's will. (2) To tell no one of our difficulties.

The next morning, the sun seemed to rise pale and reluctant and then hide itself behind some sullen clouds. I felt the same way. I didn't want to face the reality of what Sam and I had planned. Dutifully I dragged myself out of bed to get the kids up and dressed and to prepare breakfast. Later, with a kiss on the cheek and what I hoped was an encouraging smile, I bade Sam good-bye as he left on his rounds of job hunting.

After he was gone and Tiffani was occupied with her toys, I put the baby to bed. Then the morning seemed to come to a standstill.

I sat slumped in a kitchen chair. The knot that had been dispersed the night before as Sam and I prayed and read the Bible together was beginning to twist and turn in my stomach again. The sight of my two children so innocent and carefree seemed unbearably sad. Thank God they didn't know what I did! On the verge of defeat I prayed, *Lord, I have to admit that fear is as large as faith inside me. Please help!*

For the next few hours I seemed snared in a web of depression. The more I struggled, the more entangled I became. Then, the phone rang. It was Pat. We were not close friends, just casual church acquaintances, and I hadn't spoken to her for months.

"Brenda," she said, "for some reason I just can't get you and Sam off my mind. I know it sounds crazy, and please forgive me if I'm being pushy, but I just know there's something wrong. Please tell me what it is."

For a few moments I was dumbstruck. I groped for words. "No—no. There's nothing, Pat, really . . ."

"Please tell me what's wrong." Her voice was gentle but unyielding. Slowly I sort of melted, relief poured through me. To share our problem with Pat would not be breaking our second rule about telling people—obviously she already knew!

"Sam and I have no money," I began. I told her the whole story, my reluctance diminishing to nothing. She listened sympathetically.

"I just know God is going to see you through," Pat said. "I'll pray for you . . . but remember, *He cares.*"

"Oh, Pat, I feel a little more hopeful now. Thank you for calling."

After we hung up, I had a funny yet certain confidence that God was truly, this very minute, watching over me and my family, that He did care. Certainly if this mere acquaintance had intuited our problem somehow, then God knew about it in fine detail. The call seemed to be His way of telling me so. What a blessed relief! I felt more able now to carry through with our plan to follow God's will in absolutely everything, no matter what. That phone call got me through the day. And Pat followed up with a visit, and brought along some groceries.

A few days later, I looked through the food supply: a few vegetables, several jars of baby food, a can of soup, and, in the freezer, two roasts. As I fought off the mild panic that once more assailed me, the phone rang again.

"This is Diane," the voice of the church Sunday school teacher came over the line. "Judy is sick, and the class is getting a meal together to take to her. Can you make the meat dish?"

Why me? I thought. Surely almost *anyone* else in the church could more easily spare food! Judy herself—though sick—probably had a well-stocked freezer!

I opened my mouth to ask if there was someone else who could do it this time when suddenly I remembered rule No. 1: What is God's will? The answer came to mind with lightning speed—*give when you are asked to give* (Matthew 5:42, NEB). There were no qualifications to that command. Don't quibble or rationalize, just give!

"Will a roast do?" I asked.

Later, as the meat sizzled loudly in the hot skillet, I was again assailed by doubts and, worse, guilt. Was it right for a mother to reduce a family's store of food almost in half to give to someone else? But doggedly I prepared the dish, determined to stick to my part of the deal. It was an act of faith, nothing more, nothing less. "Seek ye first the kingdom of God," I repeated to myself a few times as I prepared and delivered the roast, "and all these things shall be added unto you."

Yes, Lord, I know, I prayed. *But when?*

The following Sunday, Sam and I were in the church nursery picking up Chad. I was trying not to think about what we'd eat when we got home. The second roast was gone. One can of soup?

Just then a friend, Carol, came by and, without speaking, placed an envelope in my hand. Before I could say anything, she disappeared. Sam and I just looked at each other. Then I ripped the envelope open and looked inside. "Sam," I said, "how much money do we have?"

He sighed, dug into his pockets and counted coins. "Thirty-nine cents."

I showed him the contents of the envelope. "We now have fifty dollars and thirty-nine cents."

"Thank God!" he said, and we hugged each other with tears in our eyes.

"Let's stop at the supermarket on the way home," I said.

After a joyous dinner, Sam gave thanks. "Father, more than ever I'm aware that You Yourself have given us our daily bread. Thank You. But if it be Your will, help me to find a job soon."

Two Sundays later the fifty dollars was gone. This time I was in the Sunday school room right before the service began, alone except for another woman. Then one of the ministers walked up to me and handed me an envelope. "I'm supposed to give this to you," he said.

"Who's it from?"

"I was asked not to say."

In the sanctuary, before church began, I opened the envelope. I counted one hundred fifty dollars in cash! A deep wave of God's love washed over me, and I lifted up to Heaven praise I never knew I had in me to give. I was so deeply grateful for the love and caring of our congregation—and for the sensitivity with which they remained anonymous donors. It is hard, I realized, to receive charity! But to me it meant experiencing the sufficiency of God in ways I'd only read of in books—in ways I'd never dreamed would happen to *me*.

From January to March we stretched that one hundred fifty dollars plus two paychecks totaling four hundred dollars that finally cleared the bank. Sam still could not find a job. During that time, prayer and the study of God's Word saw me through.

In the middle of March, just when our money began to give out, a man for whom Sam had occasionally worked in the past called to ask if he'd be interested in managing his shoe store. Sam accepted immediately and within a week earned his first paycheck. How we celebrated that day! And together we reflected on this astonishing fact: during our crisis, God gave us exactly what we needed, truly our *daily* bread.

As Sam and I read the Bible today, we turn the fragile pages with a new awareness: God is faithful, worthy of utter trust in the most desperate situations. As the Apostle Paul wrote: "He did not spare his own Son, but gave him up for us all; and with this gift how can he fail to lavish upon us all he has to give?" (Romans 8:32, NEB). How true these words are. But I never felt their truth until I had a desperate need.

The Deadly Snow

Sara Nealy

Winds shrieked around us, the raging snow advanced on our lonely car like an other-worldly figure in a billowing white shroud. Inside the sedan, I held Nina Lou, our sixteen-month-old baby, on my lap, while three-year-old Richie snuggled between his father and me. Richard struggled at the wheel, veering to the left, skidding to the right, charging through shallow drifts only to face larger barriers of snow.

It was January and we were on a desolate highway in the Nebraska plains. A hundred miles ahead was the town of Gordon, where Richard had a wonderful new job. We were a southern family from the Panhandle of Texas, and this was our first experience with the treacherous winter storms of the north. And we'd been so foolish! Snow had been falling this morning when we left our hotel, but the radio report had said the road north, our road, was open to traffic; the wind seemed to be dying, too. "Let's go for it," Richard had urged.

I was anxious to get to our new home. "Yes," I said, "I'm sure we'll be all right."

I couldn't have been more wrong. Though we made good time for a while, the flakes began falling faster, the wind picked up, and we no longer saw other cars on the road. Now the snow was storming around us, swirling and howling like an angry thing with flaying arms and flowing robes of tattered white. I looked away from Richard's tense face so he wouldn't see the naked fear on my own. "Should we turn back?" I asked.

"We *have* to go on." His voice was grim. "If we try to turn around, we'll get stuck for sure."

The words were barely out of his mouth when I felt the momentum of the car falter, its writhing and straining-forward motion subsiding into a gentle rocking and finally a full stop. We were locked in the deadly grip of the snow.

For a few minutes, we sat mutely in the comfortable warmth of our car, the engine and heater running, the gas indicator pointing almost to "Full." Then Richard turned off the switch. "We must ration the gas to run the heater," he explained calmly. "It may have to last us a long time."

Instantly the cold began to penetrate. We huddled together, Richie and Nina Lou between us. Richard and I took off our coats and layered them over the four of us for insulation.

After about an hour, Richard flipped the radio on. "It's a full-scale blizzard," said the local newscaster. "The temperature is now zero and falling, the wind out of the north at eighty-five miles an hour."

"It's time for heat," said Richard. He turned the ignition key.

A lifeless click hung in the air. He tried again. Again. Our eyes met. The cold motor was dead. We didn't say what we thought: *Cold. Dead.*

At that moment, I gave up hope, like a drowning person who doesn't know how to swim. The children were asleep. Exhausted by fear and tension, I joined them.

I was awakened by Richard's shaking me. "Sara, you really shouldn't sleep, you know," he said softly. "We must stay awake."

I didn't want to open my eyes to our bleak world. But suddenly, unbelievably, I felt a trace of warmth. Richard had a little fire going! He had used an aluminum coffeepot we had tried to return to friends just before leaving home. They had insisted we keep it, and now, by cutting holes with his pocketknife for ventilation, he had converted it into a mini-stove. His source of fuel was the thick blueprint mailing tubes, stacked high on the back seat, that his company had asked him to take along to his new headquarters. He had whittled cardboard chips into the pot and lit them with matches he just happened to pick up when we left the hotel.

As this evidence of God's provision dawned on me, my hope was restored. We had acted unwisely—recklessly—but God had prepared us to survive! The small fire wasn't enough to warm my physical body, but it kindled my spirit—and that made a crucial difference. I remembered the words of Jesus: "Lo, I am with you alway, even unto the end of the world" (Matthew 28:20).

Night settled around us. While Richard kept vigil over the fire, I made sure everyone stayed covered and tucked in. And the night was finally over.

The children woke up happy. Richie tugged my sleeve. "Look, Mommy, our own snow! Can we have some?"

Sure enough, right before us on the dashboard, snow had sifted in to form a little snowbank. "No, you mustn't eat it," Richard said quickly.

Nina Lou was wiggling excitedly and laughing as her little pink fingers eagerly begged.

"Why not, Richard?" I interceded. "They haven't even had a drink in twenty hours."

He hesitated. "I'm afraid it will make them sick."

"But the snow's there in front of us, almost as if God provided it. Surely His clean snow can't hurt us!"

Richard relented, and I made tiny snowballs, bite-size so we wouldn't have to hold them long. They tasted so good! Afterward, of course, there were bathroom needs. How should I handle it? We had long since become too cold to shiver, and every unit of body heat had to be preserved. At my suggestion, Richard moved the little stove closer and I eased one child at a time down beside it. As I looked at the floor of the car wondering what to do about the puddle, it turned to ice before my eyes! I'd known it was cold in the car, but this visible proof was shocking.

The hours wore on slowly, and with each one, our chance of being rescued grew more remote. According to the radio, the wind continued at ninety miles an hour and the temperature was seventeen degrees below zero. Newscasts reported all roads impassable and mentioned increasing numbers of fatalities—people who had been crossing the road to help neighbors, farmers going to their barns to check livestock. We stopped listening.

Again the swirling white-gray sky darkened into night. Richard was very still now; our fuel supply had given out, so he had no fire to tend. I kept a steady watch, rewrapping and tucking our coverings so each piece would provide maximum warmth. No one had spoken for some time. Then Richie broke the silence. "Mommy, know what I want? When we get home, I want some bread and butter and mashed potatoes with gravy."

"I'll fix it for you, darling," I whispered. "I'll fix it every day."

With that as a bedtime story, he closed his eyes and went to sleep.

It was the first and only mention of food. For more than thirty hours, the children had been as quiet as hibernating bear cubs, not even showing signs of hunger. I saw this too as God's provision, sparing me a mother's anguish of seeing her children in want. I felt God's love and concern for my children, and I thanked Him with deep gratitude. But I knew we couldn't survive much longer.

To keep my thoughts from sliding into despair, I went back over the past thirty-six hours, remembering how God had provided for our needs during each one of them. *God wants me to believe He will deliver us out of this storm*, I mused. And then I began to pray aloud: "Father, if You want to save us, I believe You can. *And I believe You want to.* But You will have to do something quickly. We can't make it till morning without heat."

I didn't hear a word, but His reply, in my mind, was perfectly articulate: *What would you have Me do?*

I thought about it. "Well, I guess first You would have to stop the wind. Yes, You would have to stop the wind because the only thing that can come through this snow is a big plow and they don't send those out on the highway until the wind stops."

At that instant, I *knew* in the depths of my soul that God was listening. I wasn't just talking to myself. The very God of the ages was with us. There was an eerie stillness, a silence as loud as a shout. *God had stopped the wind!*

My heart went wild with excitement, but I made myself go on in a quiet voice. Richard was asleep and I didn't want him to think I was suffering delusions. "Now, Lord, please nudge those men who run the snowplow. I know it's past midnight, but don't let them give up. I know there are lots of roads, but send them straight to us."

My thoughts raced ahead. Snow had nearly buried our car. If our rescuers didn't see us, they might run into us. *Well,* I thought, *I'll just have to listen for their chains. That's how I'll know they're coming. When I hear the chains, I'll turn on the car lights.* I sat there imagining how I would hear the chains clinking on the highway, hearing the first faint sounds, straining to be sure, listening with satisfaction as they grew louder, closer—then jumping to turn on the lights.

I replayed these events again and again, until the cold interrupted my reverie. A heavy aching had taken hold of me, squeezing the last remnants of warmth from my body. I could feel ice creeping up my backbone, and with it a terrible lethargy. I wanted to surrender to it.

"Father," I prayed, "I don't know if I can hold on much longer, but I can't give up because I believe. I believe You are working right now to bring help. Just make them hurry."

Again I heard the resonant clinking of the chains on the road, such a pleasant, rhythmic sound, so nice to think about.

"Father, I'll tell everyone of Your greatness. I will tell them that You care. I will tell them that *You are able.* I will tell them."

The clinking kept getting louder—such a happy sound to go to sleep by—louder, louder!

Sara, wake up! It's real! Turn on the lights!

I sprang for the light switch. "Wake up, Richard, wake up," I shouted.

The snowplow pulled up behind us. The men came bounding through the snow, shouting and laughing, clanging their shovels, throwing snow recklessly in huge scoops to get to the car. They wrenched the doors open, cheering and crying, hauling us out of the car, doing our rejoicing for us. We were like zombies, our bodies too cold to move, but they shoved us along toward safety, chattering out their elation at finding us alive.

We were the only ones. They had found more than fifty people dead.

It was nearly 2:00 A.M. Our rescuers told us how they had wanted to give up; it had been a gruesome day for them—a nightmare. But the dying of the wind had been like a command: *Go and find survivors.* Just as they were ready to go home—at the very time I had asked God to nudge them—they'd felt compelled to go out again.

So the great plow had come with rescue cars following slowly behind—warm little islands of comfort, stocked with food, fruit, thermos jugs of hot coffee, even milk for the children.

I fell asleep in the back seat of one car, Richard in another. Hours later I was awakened by an angelic voice. It was Richie, singing "Jesus Loves Me," and the sun was shining on an unbelievably beautiful world of white.

I had seen God's provision for our needs in a time of mortal danger. I had asked Him to sustain us. I had believed in His power to deliver us. And He did. God is faithful.

I will never, ever be the same.

Faith
Follows Through
on God's Directions

───────────────────────── ❧

God's Demands

Author Unknown

He never asks me to go anywhere
    He has not gone,
To face anything He has not faced,
To love anyone He does not love,
Or to give anything He has not given.

A Long, Long Way

Donna Chaney

Through the living room window of our southern Illinois home, I watched our fifteen-year-old son, Jay, trudge down the walk toward school. I was afraid that he might turn out into the snow-blanketed fields to hunt for his lost dog again. But he didn't. He turned, waved, then walked on, shoulders sagging.

His little beagle, Cricket, was missing.

Ten days had passed since that Sunday morning when Cricket did not return from his usual romp in the fields. Jay had worried all through Sunday school and church and, that afternoon, had roamed the countryside searching for his dog. At times, during those first anxious days, one or another of us would rush to the door thinking we had heard a whimper.

By now my husband, Bill, and I were sure Cricket had been taken by a hunter or struck by a car. But Jay refused to give up. One evening as I stepped outside to fill our bird feeder, I heard my son's plaintive calls drifting over the winter-blackened oaks and syca-mores lining the fields near us. At last, he came in, stamped the snow off his boots, and said, "I know you think I'm silly, Mom, but I've been asking God about Cricket and I keep getting the feeling that he's out there somewhere."

Tears glistened in his blue eyes, and he ducked his head as he pulled off the boots.

I wanted to hold him close and tell him that he could easily get another dog. But I remembered too well the day four years before when we brought him his wriggling black-chocolate-and-white-col-ored puppy. The two of them had become inseparable. And though Cricket was supposed to sleep in the laundry room, it wasn't long before I'd find him peacefully snuggled on the foot of Jay's bed. He was such a lovable little fellow, I couldn't complain.

However, in the days since Cricket's disappearance, an unusu-ally heavy snow had fallen. The temperatures were very low. I felt sure that no lost animal could have survived.

Besides, I had my own worries. Bill and I had just committed ourselves full time to a real-estate business venture. With skyrocket-ing mortgage interest rates, it was probably the worst time to be entering the field. I'd often lie awake at night worrying about it.

Here we were in our late forties, having sold a thriving dry-cleaning business, stepping into perilous waters.

Jay had helped his father remodel our new offices. And whenever he heard me express my concern, he'd glance up from his painting, smile, and say: "Don't worry, Mom, the Lord is with you."

That was Jay, all right. We all attended church regularly; even so, Bill and I often wondered where he got his strong faith. Perhaps the blow of losing a much-loved older brother in an auto accident when he was six turned Jay to the Lord for help. In any case, I'd often find him in his room, reading the Bible, Cricket curled up at his feet.

Now a week and a half had passed since Cricket had disappeared. I told Jay that I felt there was such a thing as carrying hope too far.

Looking out the window, he said, "I know it seems impossible, Mom, with the snow and all. But Jesus said that a sparrow doesn't fall without God knowing it. And," he looked at the floor, "that must be true of dogs, too, don't you think?"

What could I do? I hugged him and sent him off to school. Then I drove over to our real-estate office where I forgot all about missing dogs in the hustle of typing up listings and answering the phone. The housing market seemed to be in more of a slump than ever, and mortgages were becoming an impossibility. I glanced over at my husband, who was trying to work out some kind of financial arrangement with a forlorn-looking young couple, and wondered if any of us would make it.

The phone rang. It was Jay.

"They let us out early, Mom—a teachers' meeting. I thought I'd hunt for Cricket."

My heart twisted.

"Jay," I tried to soften the irritation in my voice, "*please* don't put yourself through that anymore. The radio here says it's ten above zero, and you know there's no chance of . . ."

"But, Mom," he pleaded, "I have this feeling. I've got to try."

"All right," I sighed, "there's a pie I baked on the stove. Help yourself to some of it before you go."

I turned back to typing up the listings. Then a contract went through my typewriter before I realized that the afternoon sun had left our office window. I hoped Jay was back home now watching television or doing his homework.

But he wasn't at home. Instead, he was still out hunting for Cricket.

After our phone call, he had put on his boots and taken off through the field where he and Cricket used to go. He walked about a half mile east and then heard some dogs barking in the distance. They sounded like penned-up beagles, so he headed in that direction. Crossing a bean field, he came upon a snowmobile someone had left sitting there. He looked it over and started walking again. But now, for some reason he couldn't determine, he found himself walking *away* from the barking.

Then he came to some railroad tracks. Hearing a train coming, he decided to watch it pass. The engineer waved at him as it roared by. With a boy's curiosity, he wondered if the tracks would be hot after a train went over them. So he climbed up the embankment and felt them; they were cold, of course.

Now, he didn't know what to do. He pitched a few rocks and finally decided to walk back down the tracks toward where he had heard the dogs barking earlier. As he stepped down the ties, the wind gusted and some hunters' shotguns echoed in the distance.

Then it happened.

Something made Jay stop dead still in his tracks. It seemed as if everything became quiet. And from down the embankment in a tangled fence-row came a faint sound, a kind of whimper.

Jay tumbled down the bank, his heart pounding. At the fence-row he pushed some growth apart and there was a pitifully weak Cricket, dangling by his left hind foot, caught in the rusty strands of the old fence. His front paws barely touched the ground. The snow around him was eaten away. It had saved him from dying of thirst.

My son carried him home and phoned me ecstatically.

Stunned, I rushed to the house. There in the kitchen was a very thin Cricket lapping food from his dish with a deliriously happy boy kneeling next to him.

Finishing, he looked up at Jay. In the little dog's adoring brown eyes I saw the innocent faith that had sustained him through those arduous days, the trust that someday his master would come.

I looked at my son who, despite all logic, went out with that same innocent faith and, with heart and soul open to his Master, was guided to his desire.

And I *knew* that if Bill and I, doing the best we could, walked in that same faith, we too would be guided through strange and circuitous paths. For how can anyone fail if he but heeds the words of the Prophet Isaiah: "And though the Lord give you the bread of adversity and the water of affliction, yet your Teacher will not hide himself. . . . And your ears shall hear a word behind you, saying, 'This is the way, walk in it,' when you turn to the right or when you turn to the left" (Isaiah 30:20–21, RSV).

The Gift That Grows

Barbara Reynolds

On the night of January 26, 1969, I embarked on a new experiment of faith, one that has changed my life. I made the following notation in my journal: "This year, I will tithe everything I receive—in wages, royalties, or gifts."

It seemed like a preposterous thing for me to do at that time because I was going through a period of great financial insecurity. After eighteen years abroad, mostly in Japan, I had resigned my position to go to the United States for a term at Pendle Hill, a Quaker study center near Philadelphia.

There was just one difficulty—I didn't have money for the fare to the United States much less enough to live there until I could find a job. And frankly I was scared! I knew I could always earn a living in Japan by teaching English. But what kind of job was there in my own country?

So it seemed a ridiculous time to begin giving a tenth of my income to the Lord. Yet the challenge had come several times over the past months in my reading, particularly the passage in Malachi 3:10 (RSV):

"Bring the full tithes into the storehouse, that there may be food in my house; and thereby put me to the test, says the Lord of hosts, if I will not open the windows of heaven for you and pour down for you an overflowing blessing."

That first night I began by adding up all the money I had in the world: a few thousand yen in a Hiroshima bank, a couple of hundred dollars in the U.S., and some small change in my purse. I figured out a tenth of all of this and, the next day, withdrew enough from my local account to make up my "purse for the Lord."

I also drew up a set of rules, which I noted in my journal:

1. Immediately upon receipt of any income, my tithes must be set apart in my special purse.

2. The tithe, from the moment I receive the income and set aside the tenth, is not mine. It is God's. Therefore when the collection plate is passed at any church, I do not give Him what is already His. I give *more*.

3. Any contributions to action groups or peace efforts (even if church-affiliated) must be over and above the basic tenth.

4. I will speak about this one-year experiment only to those to whom God requires me to speak, for the purpose of furthering the experiment and never to boast.

5. I will keep a careful record of all amounts received and given. I will note visible outward results and all felt inward growth.

On January 27, I made my first report: "The first observed result of tithing is that I realized I am far richer than I had thought. Adding up all I possess makes me realize how adequate it is—and that setting aside the tenth part for God fills me with thanksgiving and pleasure, mixed with surprise that I can do so much. Up to now I have been truly *self*-employed. Now I must become God-employed."

January 31: "An unexpected income tonight from an English class at the YMCA where I served as a substitute. I found myself thinking at once of the joy of adding something to the Lord's purse and could hardly wait to get home to make my offering."

February 7: "My account book records a succession of generous gifts on the part of friends—oranges, eggs, a quart of honey, five pounds of rice. I must also tithe such riches, finding ways to share fruit and cakes with others, lest I have too much. Surely tithing helps us avoid grasping things too firmly—an automatic self-tax as distinguished from taxation imposed by temporal authorities.

"And now—the amazing news of a foundation grant—$1000 to take care of my transportation back to the States and my expenses while studying and writing! 'Cast your bread upon the waters . . .' " (Ecclesiastes 11:1).

February 9: "She was an old woman in faded-blue work trousers, towel tied over her head, work-roughened hands pushing a wooden cart filled with buckets of oysters, mussels, and clams. But I spoke to her in Japanese—and suddenly she became a person, excited, voluble! She was a survivor of the Hiroshima bombing, and had lost her husband and two children. Now she lived with an unmarried daughter. She reduced the price of oysters by ten yen and insisted on presenting me with a plastic sack full of tiny shell-fish for soup! How does one tithe a sackful of clams?"

When it was reported in the newspaper about my return to America, letters began to pour in, many of them enclosing *osenbetsu*, farewell gifts of appreciation. My purse for the Lord became heavier and heavier, and my heart was filled to overflowing with gratitude and love. Incredible as it may seem, by the time I left Japan on March 23, I had put aside in tithes more than I had possessed to begin with, on that day less than two months before when I began my experiment!

Now, a year later, I can report that the experiment has developed into a way of life that has opened up undreamed of potential. First, it has completely freed me of the panic that used to grip me when I faced the possibility of being penniless and without a job. It has, in fact, given me such complete confidence that my needs will be met that I am now preparing to leave the part-time job security that I have enjoyed here at Pendle Hill for several months in order to devote my entire time to the writing that I feel the Lord is calling me to do.

In addition, tithing has helped me understand the joy of being a channel through which blessings can flow to those around me. The Lord's purse has been used for regular contributions to my Friends Meeting and, in addition, to help support a ghetto church whose four unpaid ministers are doing the Lord's work under very difficult circumstances.

It is not only money that continues to pour in, but friendship and loving gifts of all kinds. "Freely ye have received, freely give!" (Matthew 10:8) has become a joyous reminder that I, who one short year ago felt myself insecure and impoverished, have discovered through tithing that I have more than enough to support my own life and to give to those in need.

Above all, I have been given faith to step out with more confidence in testing the word of God. His blessings await not those who merely listen to sermons or give their solemn approval to familiar words of Scripture, but to those who will hear and obey.

Why I Quit the Gas Company

Bill Bair

I sat in a pew near the rear of the church on that October night in 1967, thinking back over my life and feeling—well, satisfied. I looked at my family sitting alongside me, my wife, Marilyn, and the five kids. The three oldest were foster children whom we'd had since they were tykes: Ted, Marlene, Judy, all teenagers now. I thought of our cottage at the seashore and the fun we had there every summer. Not bad for a guy who flunked two grades before he ever finished grammar school.

I was the kid everyone said would never make it. I never did get past the ninth grade at school, then bummed from job to job. At twenty-five I was digging ditches.

And here now, at forty-two, I had a good job in sales with the People's Natural Gas Company in western Pennsylvania, already thinking about the day when Marilyn and I would retire, buy a home in Florida, fish, travel . . .

Bill, I want you to work for Me.

That thought cut across my self-congratulations as sharply as though a voice had spoken. I was so startled I actually glanced behind me. I'd heard of God "speaking" to people, but—to me?

"Gee, Lord," I stammered, "I—I do work for You, don't I? Look at the Bible class I teach Sundays. And the youth work so many nights."

I want you full-time.

The preacher, Leonard Evans, climbed into the pulpit and started speaking, but all I heard was the uproar in my own mind. "I've got a full-time job, Lord—with the gas company! About as much job as a guy like me can handle."

Quit the gas company.

Quit the—with five kids to support! Now I knew I was hearing things. "Lord Jesus, this can't be You talking. Look at the kids!"

Look at the kids . . . suddenly, without any conscious will in the matter, I was seeing them. Not only ours but faces of kids I'd never seen. Dozens of them—frightened or rebellious or withdrawn—kids who were never going to make it.

Look at them, Bill. My children have no homes.

Interesting idea. To offer a home to such kids—not just the

appealing, moldable little fellows, but to the older ones—the ones who'd been in trouble—the ones nobody wanted. It would make a full-time job for someone. Maybe when I retired, Marilyn and I could——

Now.

"Lord, a man can't just pick up and leave that way! Look, two more years I'll be eligible for a pension. With that money we could—"

Don't you think I can care for My workers as well as the gas company can? I want you to quit your job today and I want you to go up to the front of this church and tell this congregation what you've done.

I looked around desperately, wishing the door were a few feet closer. "Lord, if this is You talking, O.K. But what if it's just some crazy idea of my own? You're going to have to give me a sign."

This was no way to talk to God Almighty, but I was too scared to care. "Lord, if this is You, have that preacher up there say my name right in the middle of his sermon."

I settled back in the pew, enormously relieved.

"Isn't that right, Bill Bair?"

Far down in front, Mr. Evans was looking straight at me. The church was tomb quiet.

"Don't you agree, Bill Bair?" he repeated.

This time as my name rang out from the pulpit I managed to reply, "Yes, Mr. Evans, that sure is right!" I had no idea what he'd been talking about. He went back to his sermon while I sat in the rear of the church knowing I was trapped.

The sermon ended with the most stirring altar call I'd ever felt. I stood and made that long walk.

At the front I turned around and, talking as rapidly as I could, said I was quitting my job and starting a home for delinquent kids and would they please pray. Then I turned back to the altar because I couldn't look my family in the eye.

I felt a hand on my shoulder. "Bill." It was Marilyn's voice. "I don't know what you're doing, but I'm with you all the way."

I turned cautiously around. Not only Marilyn but all five kids as well were standing there. And with them maybe forty other people, all of them reaching out to clap my shoulder or grip my hand.

That was the first lesson in guidance. Today, I test all nudges this way: if it's God's voice, other people will hear it too.

Monday morning I told my boss I was quitting. Well, he treated me real nice, the way you do when someone is sick. He talked about

all the legal red tape involved in chartering a nonprofit organization. It would take eight months at least. By then, you could see,
he thought I'd be all recovered.

But I began to have some tooth trouble about then, and of
course the dentist turned out to be a member of the Pennsylvania
legislature; he saw the application through personally. We had our
charter within six weeks.

A Home for Kids to me meant having a great big place, maybe
an old school building; or a farm. But as it turned out, God didn't
have that in mind at all. We first began to realize this when the
Lawrence County Child Welfare Department heard about our willingness to take troubled older children. Placement for this kind of
child, they said, was almost impossible to find. Since Marilyn and
I had already been approved as foster parents for our own three,
they wondered if we . . .

Before we knew it, Kitrick was with us; two days later, Johnny.

In a matter of weeks there were thirteen people in our family,
and still the phone kept ringing. Our own five children were wonderful, sharing rooms, moving onto sofas and bedrolls while we
borrowed cots and moved furniture around. Far from being mad
at the new turn of events, our kids were the ones who could really
get to these lonely, angry youngsters.

But all the love and furniture arranging in the world couldn't
push out the walls of the house. I was still thinking of one big
house, when one day a couple came to visit us.

"Bill, we know this is a wild idea. But do you think we could
get county approval to take in a boy like Kitrick?"

And suddenly I glimpsed His idea. God's plan, I believe, for
kids in trouble all over this nation is not another institution, but
individual Christian families opening their doors. I talked about
the new dream with the board of our nonprofit organization, and
they caught the excitement. What a troubled kid needed, we all
agreed, was Jesus. He needs to be part of a family who live their
faith, who pray together when problems come up, who lean on the
Holy Spirit's wisdom instead of their own.

And one by one, we found such homes. Here in New Wilming-
ton we started with those forty folks who were standing behind me
that October night when I turned around from the altar.

The kids come to our house first—usually straight from the
court with a probation officer to see they make it through the door.
They stay several days or several weeks while we get to know each
one's strengths and needs. Then we begin to pray for wisdom in

placing each child with the right family. One kid will need a big bunch of brothers and sisters; another should be an only child for a while.

Then we place the youngster in what we call a "love home." But in doing so we also place the child in a Christian community. For beyond the smaller community of the family there are the Christians next door in the church and throughout the entire town. Each takes a part in the child's renewal.

And as we help and pray for one another, we find that we ourselves are being helped. Families are knit together, churches reinvigorated, streets become neighborhoods. Today [written in 1971], sixty-seven families in this area are open to these youngsters; more than one hundred fifty "unwanted" kids have found homes. And the idea is spreading. Already, similar community projects are starting in Bridgeport, Connecticut, and Toronto, Canada, and several Ohio cities.

Sometimes, when I walk through the silent house late at night, checking a dozen sleeping kids, I'll remember how I kicked and struggled that night four years ago. I was like Johnny, the second little fellow who came to us. He gave us a terrible scowl as the social worker left.

"I'm only staying ten days."

"Well, that's O.K., Johnny," I said. "We'll have a real good time those ten days."

Ten days later he sidled up to me at supper. "Papa Bair?" he said. (Wouldn't you know it, Marilyn and I are Mama Bair and Papa Bair.) "Papa Bair, which comes next, fall or spring?"

"Spring," I said.

"Well," he announced, "I'm staying till fall."

You and me both, Johnny. We don't like to commit ourselves. We hang on; we make conditions. But, Johnny, once we let go, what a God He is!

The Johnstown Story

John Sherrill

My wife, Tib, bought a postcard in the gift shop at a popular overlook high above Johnstown, Pennsylvania, then joined me outside. We glanced from the picture on the card to the city below us. The photo, taken a few years before, showed smoke belching from a forest of chimneys, the blast furnaces at Bethlehem Steel spitting flames into the sky. Beneath us today, though, sprawled a silent city, its steel mills dark and cold.

And out there in ranks of hills beyond the town were the coal mines, idle too today. We could see the Conemaugh River winding between these hills, source of tragic floods, most notoriously the Great Flood of 1889.

The present emergency in Johnstown had come less suddenly than the floods, but just as cripplingly. The newspaper beneath my arm told the story. It was today's issue of the local *Tribune-Democrat* and it announced that Johnstown had the highest unemployment rate in the nation. The official figure was 22.7 percent.

And yet . . . it was another newspaper article that had prompted us to come here in the first place. A recent issue of *The Wall Street Journal* headlined some very different statistics. People were *saving* money in Johnstown at twice the national rate. The *giving* rate was up, too. As was church attendance. The divorce rate, though, had plunged. Crime too: Johnstown had the second lowest crime rate among 277 metropolitan areas across the country.

Clearly, Johnstown was finding answers in the midst of hard times, answers that the rest of us needed to know. So we'd come here to find out what those answers were, not by studying more figures but by meeting the people.

And meet them we had during the past week: businessmen and mill hands, clergymen and high school students, housewives and doctors. Almost everyone agreed on one thing: Johnstowners like Johnstown. The economy may be down, nature may be harsh, but—well, it's home. People don't leave, or if they do, they come back. "My son's working in Ohio," the lady who cleaned our hotel room told us. "But I keep his room like it is. He won't stay out there."

Commitment to a place. Not unusual in other parts of the world, rarer in America. We are descendants of people who got up and moved. The natural wisdom has been "Go west"—or south, or north—but "Go!" Only recently have experiences like that of the family who fled the recession in Illinois to find themselves still worse off, living beneath a bridge in Houston—only recently have such bad experiences with moving caused us to question this traditional response to hard times. With the frontier long vanished, with the West as populous as the East, can we still find a new beginning by moving away?

Or is the required move a spiritual one—a discovery of strengths and resources in our own backyard? This has been the experience of Johnstown, and it seemed to us that one man's story sums up what a town has learned.

His name is John Sroka. He's a businessman (real estate), fifty-seven years old, six feet tall, a hundred ninety pounds, father of four grown children.

John Sroka was eleven years old when his own father asked him to go down to Long's Garage and get some government milk. That was in 1936 and times were bad in the Conemaugh Valley. John's dad had been a coal miner until he was injured. Since then he'd worked on and off at the mills, but as the Depression deepened it was mostly off. John's dad would set out at five in the morning and come home at nine in the evening, not a penny richer. All those hours he'd have waited in the hiring hall, not daring to leave for a minute lest his name be called.

"If it hadn't been for Maggie and Jossie going dry, we still might have made it," John remembers. Maggie and Jossie were the family cows and they represented not only a steady supply of milk and butter, but an attitude. Both of John's parents came from Czechoslovakia and they brought with them some important assumptions about life and living, the most visible of which was that you could survive hard times as long as you kept on *giving*. Give to your neighbors, give to your church, give to the people across town who are less well off than you are.

Since cash was scarce, the Sroka family's giving took the form of a pound of butter to a nursing mother, a Saturday spent weeding the garden of an elderly neighbor. When John's dad was mining, he had put aside enough to start buying a house on an 80- by 120-foot lot up on the hill on a dead-end street. Here the family of nine (six daughters and John) raised enough vegetables and chickens and hogs and cows to survive. The family sold milk to the neighbors at ten cents a quart. "But if you didn't have the dime, you still got the milk."

Hog-butchering time was always sharing time. People walked away with blood sausage and headcheese and whole hams, and still, somehow, there was always enough. Giving and receiving were the same thing. When it was your turn to receive, you accepted it as part of a continuous *flow*. No one kept accounts; it was taken for granted that, when the opportunity presented itself, you would repay in some fashion.

The one thing that was not part of the flow was cash. Nobody had money and the bank wasn't interested in home-canned beans in lieu of mortgage payments. So, as hard times continued year after year, John's dad cashed in his life insurance. That supplied a thousand dollars and saved the house, but it was all the savings the family had had.

And at this point both Maggie and Jossie went dry. That was when the Srokas started thinking about the subject of the government milk. If you qualified, you could get as many as six free quarts just by showing up at Long's Garage.

"Maybe we should go," said John's mother.

John's dad never said much; he listened, he considered, then he gave his decision. He listened now. At last he turned to John: "You're the one to go."

So, as soon as he finished his early-morning job (selling papers to the few men still working at the wireworks down at the bottom of the hill), eleven-year-old John took his place in the slow-moving line outside Long's Garage.

"It was the worst experience of my childhood," John recalls. "The mood of those people waiting there was what got to me. The dole was *final.* When neighbor gave to neighbor you kept your hope. But in that milk line I knew for the first time what the Depression was."

John carried the charity milk up the hill to his home. "You can do whatever you like to me, Dad," he told his father, "but I'm never going to stand in that line again." John's dad listened, and he considered, and no Sroka ever went back to Long's Garage.

That spring, 1936, the rains were torrential. From the dormer window of his parents' bedroom John could see the Conemaugh rising steadily. One morning when he looked out, John knew there was no point setting out with his papers. The wireworks were underwater.

When the river finally returned to its banks, the people up on the hills came down, as they always did, to help those whose homes and businesses had been flooded. John's grandfather was one of those who volunteered to dig out the six feet of mud that filled St. Columba's church. It wasn't their own parish; the family went to St. Theresa's, nearer home. But John's grandfather was there, shoveling alongside the other men, when he had the heart attack. His death was saddening, but no one in Johnstown thought it unusual that a man had given his life in helping his neighbors.

Then came World War II. Steel production skyrocketed, and remained high in the post-war years. John Sroka spent two years in the Marines. On his return from the South Pacific he used his GI Bill to enroll at the University of Pittsburgh, sixty-five miles away by Greyhound bus, where he studied four days a week, returning home the remaining three to support himself and his bride, Sally (a Johnstowner, naturally), by selling houses.

Eventually John opened his own office. As his real estate business grew, he did not forget the lessons of his boyhood. "We're in the giving business," he'd tell his salesmen. "Give, give, and give some more. If you give enough, the getting will take care of itself."

With this philosophy, as the years went by, John Sroka acquired properties in various parts of the state. He and Sal and their growing family of three girls and a boy continued to live (naturally) in Johnstown. But John noticed that a subtle change had come over the city. It had begun with the war and the post-war boom. Church attendance was down, as was the interest in helping other people. The Society of St. Vincent De Paul, for instance, a laymen's organization named for a seventeenth-century Frenchman who worked among the poor, simply closed the doors of its Johnstown chapter. Who needed St. Vincent's! The economy was booming; besides, if trouble did come, the government would take up the slack.

During the 1970s both John and Sal made deeper commitments of their lives to Christ. In his prayer time John began hearing a message: *Prepare for hard times ahead.* In 1980 when the government started pulling back from its social programs, he voiced his concern to Sal.

"Things are going to be bad here in Johnstown. The next slowdown in the economy is going to leave us stranded with no help from the government and—if we don't do something about it— with no help from one another either."

But what could they do?

St. Vincent De Paul. The words came to John in his car one morning. Why not reactivate this society dedicated to helping those in need? And that was the origin of "Operation Touch," a new St. Vincent De Paul program created to help people with the problems brought on by the severe economic recession.

All over Johnstown, it was a time of almost mystic preparation, as similar nudges came simultaneously to many Christians. There are 140 churches in the greater Johnstown area. *Before* the recession started, Methodists and Byzantine Catholics and Brethren and Lutherans and others were all at work. They set up food pantries and clothes closets and family counseling centers and job referral services. Johnstown was reaching into its past to find answers to problems still in the future.

Soon, as the hard times grew harder, John and Sal Sroka found they were giving more and more time to Operation Touch. To streamline their lives and help support the various programs, they sold some of their business interests.

The more Tib and I talked to people in Johnstown, the more we saw that this kind of unselfish deed was not unusual. One man, a minister, told us that he had left a thriving pastorate to open a free-of-charge youth program. "I wanted to minister to all the young people of Johnstown," Noah Martin recalled, "but I found that a church building and denominational label had stood in my way."

Yet we found this giving attitude true of whole churches too. "Our fellowship doesn't try to keep money anymore," a chiropractor, Norman Bowers, told us, speaking about his church. "We give money out as soon as it comes in."

On and on it goes, people standing together. People pulling together where they are, rather than moving elsewhere. Love your neighbor as yourself. Jewish law commanded it. Jesus reaffirmed it. Here in this city along the Conemaugh we were seeing it happen.

The last day we were in Johnstown, Tib and I attended mass with John and Sal Sroka. The church was packed, which wouldn't have surprised us—except that it was 8:00 A.M. on a weekday. *Some special observation?* we wondered. No, no, the Srokas said. It was like this most mornings.

Why do people turn out like this in Johnstown? Well, in part to offer thanks for the sense that (at least for the near-term) better times may be on the horizon. But Johnstown isn't going to be fooled by that. Times are good and times are bad. In both, neighbors stick together. Church is where you go to hear Jesus say again that your neighbor is anyone who offers help, or needs it.

Pulling Together   *John Sherrill*

Once the idea for reactivating the St. Vincent De Paul Society came to John Sroka in his car that morning, there was a lot of work to be done. He found that two important steps were necessary before the program could be off and running. These are steps that you, too, might want to take in your community.

Step One: *"Come, tell us your need."*

When John Sroka was a boy, he knew what the needs of his neighbors were, as they knew his family's. People got together to visit and talk. Why not do the same today?

It was important, he felt, to hold get-acquainted sessions in a neutral setting; some of those who needed help had been turned off, in the past, by institutionalized religion. So John chose the Monte Carlo Restaurant, downtown, for the first meeting of Operation Touch. More than two hundred people showed up, most of them out of work. Four primary needs emerged from that night's conversations: medical help, jobs, vocational retraining, and personal counseling.

Step Two: *"Here's what help is ready now."*

John Sroka was not interested in setting up an organization that would compete with existing programs. Another gathering was called at the Monte Carlo. This time two groups were invited: the unemployed and the town's already functioning support systems. "Tell us what you have to offer," John urged the second group.

Just about every helping hand was represented at the restaurant that night. The Salvation Army, United Methodist Human Services, the various welfare programs of the state, New Day Family Counseling, Catholic Charities . . . were just a few of the groups that came and introduced themselves to the unemployed. Need and supply getting to know each other personally—hardly a new way of doing things in Johnstown.

Out of these contacts came results:

Health. A group of five busy and successful doctors donate their time free of charge to people who have exhausted other avenues to medical help. Mercy Hospital donates a suite of rooms for these doctors to use. Local pharmacists offer prescriptions free or at cost. Local dentists also volunteer services.

Want Ads. The *Tribune-Democrat* periodically offers any unemployed person free ad space in its pages.

Transportation. One of the basic needs of people looking for work is a way to get around. The Johnstown Transit Authority introduced a "Bare Fare." Available to job seekers, a ten-dollar pass allows unlimited bus rides for thirty days all over the greater Johnstown area.

Retraining. All the mobility in the world won't help if a person's skills and experience are not marketable. Operation Touch coordinates tuition-free and low-cost vocational-training programs in trade schools, computer science courses, local banks, and businesses.

TV and Radio. The local NBC affiliate has featured two half-hour specials on the how-to of getting help from your neighbors through Touch.

Emergencies. The Touch hotline is ready to put people in need—no matter what the need—in contact with a real, live person in the community who is able to help. Requests on a given day may range from help with a fuel bill to a warm coat for a school child to food for a family—available free at any of fifteen locations throughout the city. The food, the clothing, the money for the heat, all come from local neighbors and go to local neighbors.

Faith Never
Gives Up
the Dream

_____ ॐ

Seeing Beyond

Mildred N. Hoyer

See the blossom
 on the bare branch;
See the harvest
 in the tiny seed;
See the wholeness
 in the illness;
See God's Order
 in the confusion;
See Life
 in the midst of death—
See the substance
 of things unseen.

A Home of Our Own

Doug Newton

All during our college days together my wife, Margie, dreamed that someday we'd have a little house of our own. But after I finished my schooling and a three-year tour of duty as a church youth-director, she knew as well as I did that this was an impossible dream.

In the summer of 1978, I was called to be the pastor of my very first church. As August began, Margie and I packed up our bustling youth-ministry life in Syracuse, New York, along with our newborn daughter, Kelcey, and headed for western Kentucky.

The fifty-two members of "our" little church in Bowling Green couldn't pay moving expenses but offered the best salary they could. Margie and I felt that God had led us there, so I got a part-time teaching job to help make ends meet. We found a small, inexpensive apartment in a converted barn on the edge of town. There wasn't quite enough money to buy both groceries and gas, so most weeks we skimped on one or the other. Within a month's time we even had to sell our engagement and wedding rings.

Margie never complained, and her daydreams about having our own place came up less and less often, until we quit talking about them at all.

Until one day in mid-October.

I was driving home through the Kentucky countryside in our old blue Chevy, when I had the strongest conviction that we should buy a house. Since our church had had a series of short-term pastors, if Margie and I bought a house in Bowling Green, it would show our congregation we were making the kind of commitment they needed!

This sudden thought excited me as I drove up to our barn. Margie was in the kitchen with Kelcey, now nine months old. "Guess what, honey," I said. "I think we should buy a house."

The strangest look crossed her face. "Doug, we both know how impossible that seems. But today during devotions, I couldn't get the idea off my mind either!"

"I hope it's God's idea, because if it's not, we're already sunk," I said.

A few days later we found a house we liked, but I was sure we couldn't afford it. When the sales agent suggested that we apply at the bank for a mortgage loan, I hesitated. I hated to disappoint Margie, but to me it seemed a waste of time. I told Margie so.

"Doug," she said firmly, "if this is *our* idea, it's foolish. But if it's God's idea, we don't need money, we need faith."

"You're right," I agreed. "We'll call the bank in the morning."

"You understand that the application fee is nonrefundable," the bank officer intoned the next day as Margie and I sat in our best clothes, handing him the carefully filled-out form. We both thought of the fifty dollars' worth of food and gasoline we wouldn't have. Then we pictured the little house we were sure God had picked out for us. We nodded enthusiastically. "And it will take two to three weeks to process your application."

"We understand," I said. "Thanks for your time."

Our cautious optimism lasted until the phone rang the next afternoon. It was the bank officer. "Mr. Newton," he said, "I know I said it would take several weeks, but, uh, we can tell already that your financial situation isn't strong enough for us to approve your mortgage loan. If you stop by tomorrow, I'd like to return your application fee."

"Thanks." I tried to smile to myself. You had to be pretty bad off to make a bank return "nonrefundable" money!

I might have given up right then if I hadn't believed what Margie had said: "We don't need money, we need faith."

Instead, I picked up the phone and dialed a real-estate agency.

"We don't have a down payment," Margie said to the slim, pert real-estate agent that afternoon. "And we can't count on a bank for a mortgage loan."

"What you need is owner financing," she said, her sales instinct unflagging. "Don't you worry, we can find *anybody* a house. Now, how much were you planning to spend?"

We told her.

She looked thoughtful. She checked her listing file. "We do have one place at that price . . ."

What a place that was! The front porch slanted downward toward the door. There were three small rooms downstairs, with the walls all leaning in toward each other. A rickety staircase led to a room upstairs—but its ceiling was only four feet high. My dismay was mirrored in Margie's eyes.

"I don't think it's big enough," I said.

"Well, we'll call you if anything else becomes available," the agent said. We knew better than to wait by the phone. Instead, we bought all the local papers and circled every "House for Sale by Owner" in red pen.

It was the end of October when we began our search. The three of us—Margie, Kelcey and I—would load into the sky-blue Malibu. The driveway of any for-sale-by-owner house felt the tread of our tires. In each case the doorbell rang, the door opened, and the question came: "Would you be willing to hold the mortgage?" In each case, kind Southern hospitality surrounded the "No, sorry."

Finally, toward the end of November, we thought we'd found the place. The owner was willing to hold the mortgage. The price was steep for us: Thirty-seven thousand dollars. Margie and I prayed that night like never before. The answer we got seemed strange: *Offer thirty-two thousand dollars. If this is the house for you, they'll accept thirty-two thousand.*

We went back the next day. "We offer thirty-two thousand," I said.

The owner looked at us, considering. "I'll take thirty-two five."

He wouldn't budge. Neither, we decided, could we. Margie and I left, greatly disappointed. We had been *that* close!

But within a month, that little house burned to the ground. An undetected wiring problem. We felt so bad for the owner, but if we'd bought it, we would have lost everything.

The Christmas season was approaching. By scrimping every penny, we'd been able to put aside four hundred dollars for closing costs and lawyer's fees. But it was beginning to seem pointless. The house hunt was taking more energy than the church or my teaching or our family. We were both continuously exhausted.

A biting wind followed us back to the car from our last attempt. Kelcey moved restlessly in her heavy snowsuit, and Margie and I looked at each other across the car seat in the gathering winter darkness.

"Let's get something to eat," she said.

My mind was reeling as we sat in the car at Famous Recipe Chicken, eating out of the boxes in our laps. We'd both been so sure God had wanted us to find a house. So why hadn't we found one? Surely we'd been faithful to look and look and look some more. Were we wrong? Was God just trying to make us more appreciative of what we had? I'd be grateful to come home from work and, instead of running from house to house, just sit in our little apartment. I'd love to relax in one of those rocker-recliners and read the paper.

Margie pulled me away from my fantasy. "Could we have been wrong?" she asked.

"I don't know, honey."

"We've tried so hard."

I nodded. "You know," I started, "maybe we should just take the four hundred dollars and go buy a rocker-recliner."

She smiled. "We've been wanting one for years."

We munched in silence.

"We've gone through everything on the list, haven't we?" I asked.

She turned on the dome light and looked at our penned list. "There's one house left. But it's clear across town."

"Let's give it one last try. Let's check it out," I said. "Then let's go get us a rocker-recliner."

We buckled Kelcey back into her car seat and drove the five miles out of town to Hickory Lane. By now it was fully dark, so it wasn't easy to find the address. When we did, no one was home. Margie and I gave each other a meaningful look and put the car into reverse. As we swung out of the driveway, our headlights cut a white arc across a line of neighborhood houses.

Directly in front of us was a home with a small yellow "For Sale by Owner" sign tacked to a stake.

We stopped the car one final time and walked to the door.

"Would you consider holding the mortgage?" I asked the short man with white hair who answered the door.

"I reckon I could consider it," he said. "Might as well come on in, see the house, meet the missus."

For the rest of the evening we sat in the Whites' living room. We studied the beauty of the solid cherry paneling, the brick fireplace, and the built-in bookshelves. The house was wonderful. It turned out that the Whites knew one of our predecessors at the church, and they were happy to sell to us, even letting us set the payments. Our four hundred dollars held the deal; two weeks later we closed.

On a Saturday in mid-January we arrived with all of our possessions packed into a small truck. The Whites had moved their things the day before.

"Yep, everything's out," said Mr. White as he welcomed us to our new home. "Except—" he looked apologetic. "This rocker-recliner just won't fit in our new place. Mind if we leave it behind?"

Margie and I looked at the tan chair, then at each other. And suddenly we knew Who'd been most faithful of all.

Hold On

Margo Gina Hart

Just about any dream
    Grows stronger
If you hold on
    A little longer.

"I Will Not Let You Fail"

Richard H. Schneider

I am in search of a legend this gusty fall morning in Chicago. In a rental car, I pick my way around the potholes that pit these west-side streets and wonder that such a legend has flowered in this grim area.

The legend is a lady. She is teacher Marva Collins who has earned national renown for helping uneducable, school-rejected children reach fantastic levels of academic achievement.

Newspapers and magazines around the country have featured her unusual little school called "Westside Prep." A visit by CBS-TV's *60 Minutes* drew tremendous viewer response.

Seven-year-olds reading Shakespeare? Memorizing Chaucer?

Former dropouts eagerly studying Tolstoy's *War and Peace*?

Eighth-graders successfully whipping through college-level exams?

On top of this, a waiting list of some eight hundred parents anxious to get their children into Marva Collins's classes?

How does she do it? What inspired this former public school teacher to launch out on her own with a private school—an area of education usually reserved for the wealthy?

When I phoned Marva Collins, she said: "Why don't you come out and see for yourself?"

On the plane to Chicago, I reviewed what little I knew about this remarkable woman. At age forty-four, married, with three children, she had given up fourteen years of tenure in the Chicago public school system to start Westside Prep with six students in her home. That was eight years ago. Now, with five other teachers trained in her methods, she helps some two hundred youngsters progress through the eight grades in rooms in an abandoned bank building on Chicago's Madison Street.

In a day when many college graduates entering the job market have difficulty spelling, when even some best-selling authors garble grammar, the phenomenal success of Marva Collins's teaching techniques has captured the attention of educators and business leaders.

Besieged with attractive job offers ranging from superintendent of the Los Angeles school district to a high federal government post, Mrs. Collins turns them down in favor of helping under-privileged youngsters reach the fruition she feels God has intended for all children.

Obviously, it is a sacrifice to remain in this area. As I continue driving down Madison Street, corpses of autos sag at broken curbings. Unemployed men stare listlessly from doorways. A heavy spirit of hopelessness hangs over crumbling buildings.

I pull to the curb at the former bank; a drunk pounds aimlessly on my car hood, then wanders off. I wait until he turns the corner, then get out of the car.

The building entrance is neat and clean. Inside, a hand-lettered sign announcing "Westside Prep" points upstairs. I climb marble steps worn smooth by years of bank customers seeking advice on bonds and investments. In the school's reception area, a large sign proclaims another kind of investment. It reads: *Enthusiasm is the mainspring of the soul; keep it wound up and you will never be without power to get what you actually need.*

I can already sense the enthusiasm here as a teacher ushers me to a classroom where Marva Collins is at work.

There is electricity in the air as the tall, attractive teacher addresses her class in rapid-fire delivery. Her eyes flash with enthusiasm, and I see it reflected in the faces of the thirty-five students sitting raptly before her.

Glancing at me, she points to an empty chair at the side of the room. I quickly sit down, suddenly transported back to my grammar school days. I find myself engrossed in what this teacher is saying. She is in *command* of this room.

"Gaining knowledge isn't like buying a hamburger at McDonald's," she is saying. "You have to *earn* it, and earning it takes hard work."

She is talking about homework assignments. "Each and every one of you is expected to do *all* of your homework," she emphasizes. "If you don't, then you will come in on Saturday and help clean the school."

She points to assignments on a blackboard crowded with chalked diagrams of sentence structure and mathematical problems. I never was good at math, and so my attention turns to the students who now open their books to take turns reading from Chaucer's *Canterbury Tales*.

"Who can tell me when this was written?" asks Mrs. Collins. Hands shoot up. "Between 1380 and 1390," answers a girl who can't be more than ten.

Little voices enunciate the archaic English: "Whan that Aprille with his shoures sote . . ."

It sounds familiar. But wait. I was in high school when I studied that poem. Some of these kids are eight years old! And those math problems on the board. I had trouble with them as a college freshman!

Mrs. Collins snaps me to the present as she assigns a passage to memorize.

"Be ready to recite it tomorrow," she says, "and I also want you to write a theme telling what you have learned from the poem about English life in the fourteenth century."

A perplexed look on the face of a little boy in the front row catches the teacher's perceptive eye.

"Do you think you can do it, Chauncey?" she asks.

"Unh, hmmm," he nods.

"Now, Chauncey," she says as she steps closer to his desk, her voice softening, "we must always speak clearly, both in this class and elsewhere. We don't mumble, 'Unh, hmmm.' What do we say?"

"Yes," he enunciated.

"Excellent. When you speak clearly and forthrightly, people not only understand you but they respect you. Remember that, children."

She tells the boy she will be glad to help him further after class if he needs help, and the children continue taking turns reading Chaucer aloud, discussing the plot as they go.

I sit in amazement. At the same age as some of these children, my two sons were reading: *Look, look, see Jane run.*

Later Marva Collins tells me that the children read aloud in class "because it keeps them from mispronouncing words as they are likely to do if they read silently. Oral reading is beneficial to punctuation, vocabulary, and style. Children begin to understand synonyms, characterization, conflict, and the author's point of view."

As the sun slants through the big overhead skylight, one boy lays his head down on his desk.

The delivery from the blackboard halts. "Percival!"

Percival's head shoots up.

"If you want to sleep, you may go home right now and go to bed."

Percival obviously doesn't want to go home.

"I can only help you, Percival, when you pay attention."

As usual, the discipline is tempered with a loving tone. Discipline, love, and tough drilling in the basics. If I have learned anything at all about Marva Collins's schoolroom techniques so far, this is her secret—something quite common in the 1800s, when *McGuffey's Reader* covered all the basic subjects in a straightforward, moral tone. Something that seems to have been forgotten in recent years.

Challenge is something I'm also hearing, children being challenged to rise above their own expectations. In the ghetto area, expectations are usually squashed before a child even enters school.

"But it takes work," Mrs. Collins emphasizes as she drills the children on individual responsibility. "Success doesn't come to you," she says. "You go to it. You don't buy it with Green Stamps. There's no paycheck until the work is done. You don't get a report card unless all the homework is in. Every moment here must be used in a profitable way for you, by learning, learning, learning."

In one drill, when a boy admits that he knows only half his lessons, Mrs. Collins says: "When you go home, I'll ask your mother to give you only half your dinner."

Discipline varies with the need in Mrs. Collins's classroom. A youngster turns and mutters something to the student sitting behind him.

"Robert."

"Yes, ma'am?"

"If you must talk in class, you may come up here and take over as teacher."

Noticeably embarrassed, he walks with dragging feet up to the front of the class. Marva Collins hands her pointer to him and sits in his vacated chair.

In the tense interval, as Robert sheepishly stands before the class, he obviously decides that he had better pay attention from now on.

Later, other children come up before the class, this time to work at the blackboard, where they blend vowels and consonants, sound out words, and diagram sentences.

"Well-spoken English is part of your passport to success," stresses Marva Collins. "And this means not using the same words all the time. Enlarge your vocabulary. Instead of the word 'big,' learn other ways of expressing size, such as 'huge,' 'mammoth,' 'gigantic,' or 'tremendous.' "

I learn that each of Marva Collins's students is expected to read one book every two weeks, memorize one poem per week, and write one well-constructed composition a day.

After Mrs. Collins again goes over today's homework, the class session ends. Instead of a mad dash to the door, the students seem reluctant to leave. However, one small boy exuberantly leapfrogs over the back of the desk. Marva Collins is on him in an instant: "Tyrone, the Lord didn't make you a frog to go jumping around like that. He made you a handsome boy."

The little fellow glances up with a mixture of embarrassment and appreciation on his face at having been corrected on the one hand and complimented on the other. I felt sure he would not soon forget it.

The children finally file out, but one child still sits at her desk. She is buried in a book, oblivious to everything else. I catch a glimpse of the title. It is Shakespeare's *Hamlet.*

Marva Collins walks over and gently touches her shoulder. The girl, about nine years old, looks up. "Oh, I'm sorry. I didn't realize. I became so interested in reading about Polonius and Laertes that I lost track of time."

Later, as we leave the building, Marva Collins refers to her. "That's Erika; I'll tell you a little story about her later."

After a short drive I visit with Marva Collins and her husband, Clarence, in their tastefully furnished home. It is still in a rundown area but Marva Collins doesn't mind. "We don't let the outside touch the inside," she smiles.

As we talk, she tells how Westside Prep began, with a dream.

"Eight years ago I was sitting alone in my public school classroom. The closing bell had rung and the halls were bedlam with shouting, fighting children. I couldn't blame them. Who wouldn't be bored by the incredible banalities of many modern-day lessons. If their minds couldn't be occupied or stimulated, naturally they would rebel. I had learned with my own students that when I introduced them to Melville's *Moby Dick* or Emerson's *Essays,* the lofty thoughts inspired them to add their own.

"I prayed that day," she said, smiling in memory. "I asked God to help me accept the things I couldn't change and change those I could."

"And that's when my dream came to me. I dreamed of a school where children could be challenged to make full use of all the intelligence and talent that God has given them.

"Only trouble was we didn't have any money. Then I remembered my teacher's pension. So we cashed it in.

"We worried at first," she said, looking at her husband and taking his hand. "It was all we had. But we believed that if God wanted us to do it, He would take care of us."

And so all five Collinses worked, including sons Terry and Eric and daughter Cynthia, as they transformed an upstairs room into a classroom.

When September came, they set up battered, cast-off desks, assembled books retrieved from public schools' trash, and let the word out that Westside Prep was opening its doors. "We had no entrance requirements," said Marva, "other than the parents' wish for their children to excel." She added that there was a small tuition fee for those able to pay.

"But I'll never forget that first day," she laughed. "Along with the cast-off desks and blackboards, it was evident we had gotten the cast-off children.

"Almost every child had been rejected by the public schools as 'retarded' or 'troublesome.'

"That night I prayed for strength. 'How come You didn't send me the bright children, Lord?' I asked. And the answer I seemed to get was, 'All My children are bright.'

"I asked Him to help me," she added.

"The next morning, standing before the blackboard, I looked each child in the eye and told them: 'I will not let you fail. You are the brightest children in the whole world. And I want each of you to know that the words "I can't" are a lie.'

"And so it started. I learned to let each child know: I love you all the time, but I disagree with you some of the time.

"Discipline was one thing. But how could I get them to start reading? 'If you can't read, you can't do anything,' I told them. 'You can't even learn mathematics.' But I knew talk wouldn't do it. How could I get them hooked?

"I thought of the drug pushers outside who give youngsters a small amount of dope, enough to get them hooked so they'd come back for more.

"I did the same with reading by starting them out with interesting fragments from the classics. For example, I started them with the scene of the witches in *Macbeth*. Intrigued, they continued on with the rest of the story.

"And our numbers grew as more and more children eagerly came to school, even though we don't have recess and have only a short lunch break. The parents know that this is one place where nobody gets by with foolishness. They know their children will be taught to think. And they know that children who think don't get on drugs, don't rape, don't break into houses—because they feel good about themselves.

"Oh, it's not easy," she added, leaning back in her chair and brushing back her hair. "Often we have to break wooden pencils in two to have enough for everybody and use the backs of old work papers. The government offered us funds, but I couldn't accept them. We don't want to march to the federal drum; all I have to do is look at the worsening condition of my neighborhood schools despite more than ten years of government funding for new audio-visual programs and other 'teaching aids.'

"So we still limp along. We never know from week to week whether we can pay our rent on the schoolrooms. But I have come to trust the Lord in every way. Somehow, someway, and often at the last minute, we seem to manage.

"You know," she said, "when I get to feeling hopeless, I think of one of our first students. She was a seven-year-old who sat at her desk, sullen and runny-nosed. 'Can't read,' she grunted, 'other teacher say I ain't ever gonna read.'

"Later that day the little girl got down on the floor and scrunched herself out of the door. I caught her running down the street and hauled her back.

" 'You are a strong-willed child,' I said, giving her a tissue for her nose, 'but between the Lord and me, our will is stronger than yours.' "

Marva Collins leaned toward me. "You met this child today."

"Oh?"

"Erika, remember?"

I remembered; the girl who loved reading about Polonius and Laertes.

As I leave the Collinses' home, it is early evening; long shadows reach across the broken streets, and a grimy haze hangs low over the darkening buildings.

But I can understand why Marva Collins prefers to stay here rather than accept the fancy job offers in glamorous places. Jesus spoke of it: "Lay not up for yourselves treasures upon earth . . . but lay up for yourselves treasures in heaven" (Matthew 6:19–20).

I thought about the happy children who were finding the richest kind of fulfillment. Marva Collins has found her treasure.

Don't Be Frightened by Failure &

Austin Pardue

So much emphasis is placed nowadays on the importance of achieving great success in life that I wonder sometimes what becomes of all the people who sometimes have to settle for less, people who know the meaning of that grim word *failure.* How do they stand it? How do they adjust? How do they come back from the deep discouragement that failure—or apparent failure—often brings?

I think I have something to say to such people, because in my time I have had more than a nodding acquaintance with failure.

First, let me give you a text that in my opinion deserves the attention of all sincere people who meet with failure. "He bindeth the floods from overflowing; and the thing that is hid bringeth he forth to light" (Job 28:11). What are the floods, viewed in this context? They are the surging, devastating floods of defeatism and despair that so often follow failure. And what is "the thing that is hid?" That's what I want to talk about.

I started out in life as a resounding academic failure. In grammar school, where we were seated in order of our grades, I usually sat in the right rear corner seat—the lowest in the class of about forty or fifty. And I discovered that if you sit in the lowest seat long enough, you begin to have a pretty poor opinion of your future possibilities.

I had to go to summer school to get through grammar school, which must be some kind of a record for academic density. I never did graduate from high school. When World War I came along, I left school to enlist at age seventeen.

After the war, I decided I wanted to go into the ministry. I found that if you had been in the service, you could enter college without a high school diploma, so I went to Hobart, a fine old Episcopal college at Geneva, New York. I arrived there with ten dollars in my pocket. I got a job with the Lackawanna Railroad, heaving trunks on and off trains early in the morning. I went out for football—and I sincerely tried to study.

One day the president of the college called me in and said, "I'm not sure you should be here; I'm going to give you an I.Q. test." I took the test, and apparently it claimed to prove that I was about a middle-grade moron. The president called me in again and said,

"Pardue, you'll never get through college. You'll never be a minister. You just can't make it."

The next fall I tried again at Hobart, and the same thing happened. Another I.Q. test. Another disaster. The president said, "Pardue, what you should be is a farmer, or one who works with his hands [not one of my gifts]. Anyway, you shouldn't be here." So I was out for the second time.

I tried another small college called St. Stevens, and the president there was cordial. "We'll send for your credentials," he said. "I haven't any," I answered. "In that case," he said, "what makes you think you can come here?" "I don't know," I said. "I believe that God has a plan for me and maybe your college is part of it."

Well, they let me enter, but that didn't work out either. I could not make the grade. Before long I was asked to leave.

When I returned home to Chicago, I still felt that somehow, ordination to the Episcopal priesthood could and would be achieved even though I was without money, academic credentials, or powerful backers. My kindly rector just about gave up on me, but the curate at my parish church listened to my story. He told me that he had gone through a somewhat similar experience and wrote on my behalf to the dean of Nashotah House, an Episcopal seminary that had a special preparatory department for men without college degrees.

I went there and eventually the dean asked me the most important question I had ever been asked: Had I ever had a careful eye examination? I had not. He made an appointment with an oculist in Milwaukee who was amazed that I could study at all. My vision was very good, but my muscular focus almost nil, a condition later diagnosed as dyslexia. I was given a prism, and did endless exercises. A burden of inferiority was lifted. Since grade school I had been convinced that I must be stupid.

So I kept going—I believe it was really because my mother sincerely believed that "with God all things are possible" (Matthew 19:26) and she somehow conveyed this belief to me. Finally I did learn to study and I did graduate from a theological seminary and I did become an Episcopal priest and later a bishop.

I am sure God has a sense of humor, and you can see it in the first chapter of First Corinthians, verse 27, where Paul says: "But God hath chosen the foolish things of the world to confound the wise; and God hath chosen the weak things of the world to confound the things which are mighty." Now forgive me, I'm not boasting, but today, even without high school or college diplomas,

I have five honorary doctoral degrees, and have published ten books—which proves that God has a sense of humor.

But I also think it proves something else, which brings me to the remainder of that text about "the thing that is hid." I think the thing that is hid very often is a gift that the individual has that he or she doesn't even suspect having. No matter how low an opinion of yourself you may have, the Bible will tell you that there are all kinds of gifts and each of us has some of them. In my case, I had a gift, but it was hidden behind my eye trouble until the Lord decided to bring it to light.

I think that all of us should remember this when failure strikes, or seems to strike. Just because you fail at one thing doesn't mean that you will fail at another. The word *education* comes from a Latin word meaning "to draw out"—not necessarily to cram full of facts and information and dates, although these too can be important. Education really means to draw out the mysterious hidden qualities within an individual, to bring them forth "into the light."

The truth is, there are many things an I.Q. test can't tell you. It can't measure how much creative imagination a person has, or how much drive, or how much burning desire to do or be something. It can't determine how much willingness a person has to cooperate with other people, or how much latent leadership he or she has, or how much perseverance he or she may possess. These are gifts of God.

So seek your gift, and keep looking for it diligently. Don't let failure discourage or dishearten you. Sometimes the way is long, painful, and hard, but by the grace of God, and with a belief in the guidance of His Holy Spirit, He will show you how it can be done.

Full Blossoming

Josephine Millard

As tight-closed buds that feel the sun
Burst forth in perfect bloom,
Drab, stinted lives will blossom forth
When God is given room.

Rough Road to Moscow

Simon Estes

As I grew up, it never entered my mind that one day I'd become an opera singer. I thought about being a minister, a social worker, or a doctor—but even those were pretty unusual plans for a kid from our integrated, blue-collar neighborhood in Centerville, Iowa. In fact, I was almost through college with a degree in social work when my voice teacher, Charles Kellis, sat me down.

"Simon, I think you could sing opera."

"What's opera?" I asked blankly. Sure, I knew it existed. I'd just never paid any attention.

In response, he started giving me records of the great opera singers. In no time I was hooked. Where once I'd never dreamed of being an opera singer, I suddenly dreamed of nothing else. When my rational mind insisted that the odds against becoming successful at it were overwhelming, my heart would counter with the strong faith I'd received from my parents. My father worked hard as a coal miner, porter, and chauffeur to give us the education he'd missed. Even in lean times he'd taught us that if we had faith, God would supply our needs.

"If you believe in God, Son, and believe in yourself, there isn't any challenge you can't meet."

Well, I *did* believe in God, and I *did* believe in myself. So I accepted the challenge of becoming an opera singer, confident that God would provide what I really needed.

Things came easily at first. In 1964 I won a scholarship to study voice at the Juilliard School in New York. Then I was advised to start my career in Europe, where large roles are more readily available to newcomers. In 1965 I auditioned for the Deutsche Oper in West Berlin, and within a month I was singing the bass lead of Ramfis in Verdi's *Aïda.* From there I moved to other German opera houses, determined to learn new roles and increase my repertoire.

But I soon discovered that in Europe big roles and good reviews don't necessarily put bread on the table. In fact, I was flat broke. But I was determined not to give up.

One friend suggested that I apply for a stipend from the Institute of International Education in New York. I'll admit I was doubtful. If I'd never heard of them, certainly they'd never heard of me. Why should they help me out?

Much to my surprise, the man in the office I'd been directed to jumped to his feet and extended his hand.

"Simon!" he said. "What a pleasure to meet you! You won the Munich Competition last year, didn't you? How would you like to compete in the Tchaikovsky Competition in Moscow?"

Would I! I was flabbergasted. The Tchaikovsky Competition is a very prestigious event held only every four years. Winning it has brought international attention to young artists, almost assuring successful careers in opera, piano, violin, and cello. Our American Van Cliburn wasone of the first piano winners, in 1958. And look at *his* career!

"Sure I'd like to go," I said quickly, but added honestly, "There just isn't any way I can afford to get to Moscow."

"That would be taken care of. We'd pay your way over, and the Competition would pay your way back. You'd need to prepare several Tchaikovsky songs in Russian, but we'd provide funds for you to learn the language. If you can go, let me know, and we'll make arrangements."

I immediately checked with the manager of the opera house in Lübeck, Germany, where I was under contract. He readily agreed to let me go to Moscow.

Thrilled, I flew back to Lübeck. Where I'd hoped for a small stipend, I'd been given the chance of a lifetime.

But as the summer—and the Competition—approached, *everything* went wrong. First, through some unavoidable snags, the money for me to study Russian never materialized. I wired New York again, then stopped by the impressive office of the manager of the Lübeck opera house.

"Good day," I said in German, "I just wanted to remind you that I'll be leaving next month for the Tchaikovsky Competition in Moscow."

His answer was curt. "You can't go."

"But you agreed! Arrangements have been made!"

"I've changed my mind," he growled. "If you go, not only will you be fired, you'll never work in Germany again!"

There was no changing his mind. I left his office, stunned. To lose such a chance—and for no reason! And not only was my Lübeck job on the line, but I'd had a very good offer to sing in Hamburg the next year.

At home that night I said a prayer. "Lord," I started, "if You'll just show me a teeny bit of light at the end of the tunnel, I'll gladly do the rest."

Shortly thereafter, at the opera house, I fell into conversation with a tenor from Australia. He was sympathetic and soon I'd explained my dilemma.

"I think you should go," he said in his cheerful voice with the Australian cadence. "This chance might not come again. The worst thing that could happen is that you won't get to finish out the season here in Lübeck."

"But the offer in Hamburg—"

"Have you gone to talk to them and explain the situation? There's no reason they should fire you because this manager went back on his word."

"I haven't talked to them," I said, a little embarrassed. "To tell the truth, the manager seemed so threatening that I've been afraid to leave Lübeck."

His laughter was deep and hearty. "You're an opera singer, Simon, not a criminal! Nobody's checking train stations to see if you leave town!"

His confidence reassured me. I did go to Hamburg, and sure enough, they promised me the job, no matter what. That was the glimmer of light I'd asked God for.

But by now the Competition was only days away—and I didn't know a word of Russian! I had the rest of the repertoire I'd need, and the way was provided. But there was still that brick wall. I'd have to sing in Russian in the first round, almost straight off the plane. No Russian, no chance. And I had no Russian.

There was nothing further I could do. I prayed, "God, I don't want to ask You to do any great favors for me. Please just help me as much as you feel is right."

And I started to pack.

The first of June was overcast. A strange excitement played at my stomach as I boarded the Aeroflot plane in East Berlin. In my briefcase were my reams of sheet music—including several unknown pieces with the strange symbols denoting inscrutable words in Russian. I had a facility for languages, but I could stare at those foreign pages for the rest of my life and not know how to decipher a sound. I leaned back in my seat and tried to take my mind off our imminent arrival in Moscow.

As the plane took off, I noticed the attractive, thirtyish woman assigned to the seat next to mine. Not surprisingly, I was the only black person on the flight, and she looked at me with curiosity. She said something in a language I didn't understand, and I shook my head. She didn't speak English. As a last resort, I asked if she spoke German, and she did.

"Why are you going to Moscow?" she asked in German.

"I'm going to sing in the Tchaikovsky Competition," I said, then added, "By the way, do you know any pieces by Tchaikovsky? I need to sing one in Russian when I arrive."

Her face lit up. "You ask a Russian actress if she knows any songs by Tchaikovsky?" she asked, grinning. "Let's see what music you have."

I spread out the scores that I'd brought. "Here!" she said picking one up. "This is my favorite: 'Ni Slova, O Drug Moi' ['Not a Word, O My Friend']."

All the way from Berlin to Moscow, she went over and over the Russian words and pronunciations with me, while I sight-read the music.

I'm sure the flight attendant thought we were nuts, reciting over and over, "Ni slova, O drug moi, ni slova . . ."

When I landed in Moscow, my assigned accompanist helped me put the finishing touches on the song before I was hurried over to sing in the first round. I'll never forget walking onto that stage in the Tchaikovsky Conservatory Recital Hall. It was breathtakingly beautiful and packed with expectant people. My accompanist hit those first chords of Tchaikovsky's piece, and I stepped forward and sang it—in Tchaikovsky's native tongue. After that first round, I went on to win the bronze medal—which really launched my career. True, I lost my summer position in Lübeck, but it was replaced by another offer to sing—at the White House.

But what still amazes me is that after hearing that first song, the Soviet newspaper Pravda wrote that I had the best Russian in the Competition!

Whenever I think of it, I have to grin. Because when I got on that plane with faith, God knew that as far as Russian was concerned, I knew not a word, oh my friend.

And before we landed, those were the very words I could sing.

Faith Works
for the
Impossible

Moving Faith

Mildred N. Hoyer

Dear Lord . . .
I ask not for a faith
that will move a mountain
but for a faith that will
somehow move me.

The Girl at the Gate

Vivian Moffitt

During the drought and Depression years, when I was a girl in North Dakota, my parents were farming with as little hired help as possible. All of us kids did as much as we could to help my parents on the farm. Though I had cerebral palsy, I walked fairly well and I helped with the livestock.

Each morning Dad and I drove our sixteen Holsteins through a big gate and into an alfalfa field. I stayed and watched so they would not stray. By noon they were thirsty and ready to go back into their barn. But the gate was heavy and the chain that fastened it was tight. My right hand was very spastic and my strong left one was poorly coordinated. Each day I waited until Dad came from his work to close the gate.

One day he came in from plowing, put the horses in the barn, and started for the house. I called him but he did not answer. Dragging the gate a few inches at a time, I could almost close it.

Still Dad didn't come. If the gate was left unfastened, the cows would push through and break it. I was becoming annoyed. I knew Dad was tired and hungry—but so was I.

With one more push, the gate was almost in place. Lifting my bad hand with my good one, I grasped one end of the chain. Then I pulled hard on the other end. No luck. I called for Dad again, but there was no answer. While I waited, I kept trying. I prayed, but with more self-pity than confidence. I gave one more push to the big gate, then held it in place with my knee while I tugged at the chain again. My prayer got the answer it scarcely deserved; somehow the ends came together, then overlapped so I could get the end link into the snap.

I was no longer tired. I ran to the house and fairly crowed, "Dad, you forgot to come and shut the gate, but I got it done!"

He grinned at me. "I thought you could," he answered quietly.

He had been watching from the dining room window. If I had not succeeded, he would have come to help me.

In the thirty-five years since then, I have had many of the frustrations that are common to the handicapped. Sometimes I doubted that my prayers were heard. Yet, when I kept trying to be self-reliant and useful, my struggles and even my failures eventually had meaning and purpose.

I know now that at times our Heavenly Father, like Dad, watches from inside the window, seeming to withhold His help to give us the joy of discovering the strength He has hidden in us.

Down Is a Long Way from Out

Flora Walker

It was 4:30 in the afternoon. Time for Mister Softee. I cringed at the sound of the ice-cream truck's bell. The driver stopped outside Talbot Towers, the "ghetto complex" in a western Pennsylvania town where my three kids and I had just moved. As he handed out ice pops and took dimes from a growing cluster of eager, squirming children, I gazed anxiously down at my kids from the window. They had no dimes. They hung over to the side and watched, and the hurt, left-out look in their eyes made me ache inside.

It was the summer of 1965, and we were so miserably poor we couldn't afford even an ice cream on a stick. I had just left my husband of sixteen years. He was an alcoholic, and night after night he had come home drunk and hit me as I lay in bed. Trembling and stunned, I'd run out into the street in my nightgown and wait until it was safe to creep back inside.

I tried to stifle my screams so the children wouldn't know, but I couldn't take the beatings anymore. I was afraid that he would eventually kill me. One night my husband returned to an empty house. The kids and I had left.

I had reached a point in life where I needed something to give me courage to continue—something to give me the determination to overcome my problems. I had lost my grip on life.

We lived in Braddock, Pennsylvania, a steel-mill town, and this huge, grimy apartment building with its rats and roaches and forty-two other families was where we had to start over in life. My oldest child, Kathy, was fifteen and had cerebral palsy. She stumbled and slurred her words, but what a joy she was to me. She was always smiling and soothing my temper. I scrimped out of the little money there was to buy the forty-seven-dollar soft-leather shoes and the vitamins that she needed.

Eddie, my five-year-old, was fragile and little; and Lucille, the baby, was almost four. We lived on a small Welfare grant. Although my husband was ordered by the court to contribute child support—only twenty-one dollars a week—there was never enough. Some days I fed the children cereal with milk for each meal, and I would go without. I'd lie awake at nights, doubled over with cramps from hunger.

Lying there I would be overwhelmed by despair. "Even God is deserting me. Why am I being punished?" I wondered.

I had tried for years to stay by my husband. He'd been a good provider but impossible to live with. I had tried to raise our children right, to take them to church. I had nurtured Kathy through difficult times—exercising her three times a day, boiling and mashing up her food because of her difficulty in swallowing, taking her from one doctor to another, carrying her from one class to the next when she couldn't climb the school stairs.

Now we were crammed into a tiny apartment with no relief in sight and no one to turn to. We were trapped. I began to think that my body and my life were too battered to start again. And yet, there came a point, one tiny moment . . .

One afternoon Eddie ran up all six flights of stairs and burst into the apartment. He was crying so hard he could hardly get his breath.

"Eddie!" I said. "What's wrong?"

But he sobbed uncontrollably. His shoulders drooped. He looked crushed.

I took him in my arms and coaxed, "It's all right, Eddie. You can tell me." I hugged him close and kissed his wet cheeks.

"Mother," Eddie said, choking on the words, "Mother, are you *lazy?*" He avoided my eyes, and I was glad because I didn't want him to see the hurt in mine.

"What a question to ask your mother, Eddie! Don't I take care of you and your sisters, cook and clean and wash clothes? Is that being lazy?"

"The kids outside say that you don't have a job," said Eddie haltingly. "They said their daddies have to support us. They said you don't work because you're lazy! They said we are *nothing!*"

Children, I knew, could be cruel to one another, but now the shock and hurt were almost too much for me to bear. My little remaining self-respect was stripped away, and I wanted to hide somewhere and die of shame.

That night in the darkness of my room, I went on my knees to God. I gave him all of my sadness, my anger, my hopelessness: "Life is too hard, dear Lord. I'm losing hope. Will You please help me?"

The next morning I was looking in the mirror, and I said out loud, "Well, God knows I'm not lazy." I studied myself closely. "Flora," I said, "you've still got your figure. You've got a good mind, and more skills than a lot of people have. You've got your high school diploma and all those things you learned—typing, filing, shorthand. You've got a nice personality. You're not so hopeless. So-o-o, why don't you do something about your situation?"

I knocked on my neighbor's door, borrowed her morning paper, and turned quickly to the classified section. Then I saw it: "Wanted, secretary for librarian, parochial school . . ."

I thought to myself, Maybe . . . just maybe . . . I borrowed her phone, called the listed number, and asked for an appointment. I was given one for the next morning! But if I'd known about the competition for that job, I wouldn't have been so pleased.

I arranged for someone to watch Eddie and Lucille while I was on my interview, then spent the rest of the day getting ready. I washed my hair, polished my one pair of good shoes, and looked over my scanty wardrobe. Nothing in the closet looked suitable. Just a few faded housedresses. My husband had never bought me a dressy dress.

Then I saw, hanging in the back, an old green suit. Ugh, I thought, nobody would ever hire me in that thing! It was a hand-me-down given me to wear to my high school graduation. I looked frantically from hanger to hanger, but it was that green suit or nothing. Then I decided, "I got a diploma in this outfit. I can get a job in it too!"

I spent the rest of the afternoon and evening banging out typing drills on my old typewriter and taking down radio announcements in shorthand. When Kathy came home, she sat beside me and read aloud long business letters from her typing book. She struggled over the words as I struggled over the keys, but we kept at it until late in the night.

I awoke early the next morning, and ironed my suit and checked over the rest of my wardrobe. No stockings! There was no time and no money to buy a pair, so I rushed next door to Gladys Vandiver, who lent me a pair of hers. I'd polished and curled and ironed myself into as best shape I could, and as I took a last look in the mirror, I said, "Flora, you can do it!"

I arrived at St. Thomas High School at 8:30 for my 9:30 appointment. Already there were other women waiting in the office. They were young and pretty, intelligent-looking, well-dressed—and white. And they were all waiting to be interviewed for *my* job. *Dear God,* I asked dismally, *what chance do I have?*

I was the last to be interviewed, and as I waited, I carried on a long conversation with myself. *Flora,* I told myself, *you know you are not lazy. You are a special person. What difference does it make that this school is predominantly white? What they need is you. Your talents are just as necessary as any of those other women's. You know you could contribute a lot to this job. You have high morals, dedication, and drive. You have skills, potential . . .*

By the time I walked into Father Henry's office for my interview, I had just about hired myself. I was convinced that this place couldn't do *without* me.

Father Henry, the headmaster, said, "I see you did well on the typing and vocabulary tests." Then he told me what the job required and asked if I thought I could handle the responsibilities.

"Father Henry," I assured him, "I am a woman who can deal with responsibility. I *know* I would be an asset to this library, and if you don't hire me, the loss will be *yours!*" I couldn't believe I'd said that, and I waited fearfully for the man's response.

"I like your spunk," he said, smiling. And after talking a while longer, he said, "I need a mature person. Could you start today?"

"What did you say?" I almost shouted at this huge, kind man. "Oh, yes, yes, I'll take the job. Just let me make arrangements for my children," I pleaded, and left with a bounce in my step.

That wonderful $1.25-an-hour job was a start, a new beginning, and God and I both knew I desperately needed it.

Little did I know that this was to become a springboard for my future. I stayed there six years, then worked as a secretary for a legal services organization. I also became chairman of the Metropolitan Tenants Organization, a volunteer group, in which I worked to improve living conditions for apartment dwellers. I became active in four other associations involved in improving the environment and living conditions—to try to make the world a little better place for my children.

Later I married my second husband, Christopher Walker, a fine Christian man. We have a home on fifty-four acres of land in

Anderson, South Carolina. Now I'm working in the history department of Clemson University. God knows, I have not been lazy since Eddie came crying to me that day. Life has been rich and full and rewarding and *busy*. My youngest, Lucille, finished school and married this past June; Eddie operates a forklift here in South Carolina; and Kathy is married to a minister and lives in Washington, D.C.

I remember the first afternoon home from my new job at St. Thomas High School. The children and I were gathered around the table, where I was excitedly relating the news about my job. "And I called the man at the Welfare Office and told him to stop sending checks because we won't be needing them anymore," I told them proudly.

Just then we heard the Mister Softee bell. "Come on," I said to the kids. "Let's celebrate."

And celebrate we did.

Two Men and a Plow

Claud Rodgers

My daddy, Guy Rodgers, was a weaver in a cotton mill near Griffin, Georgia, a skilled laborer with only a third-grade education. He and Mama, my two sisters, and I lived in a four-room house with a faucet outside for water. We bought our coal and electricity from the huge plant where Daddy worked, and lived a life so simple we didn't need to own a clock. Most people timed everything by the mill whistle that signaled shift changes.

"Short time" at the mill came regularly—periods when orders fell off and the plant operated only one or two days a week. In the best of times, nobody in the village had much, but short time meant disaster. Our little town offered no other jobs, so when incomes fell behind, most people bought groceries on credit. If you owed the grocer fifteen or eighteen dollars, it could take years to catch up.

Daddy refused to buy food on credit. There was a confidence in him that kept us kids from knowing we were poor. He thought he was the luckiest man in the world. He thanked God daily for his family, his job, and our home, and he prayed for less fortunate neighbors and tried to help them.

One afternoon when I was about seven, Daddy sat on the steps of our high back stoop talking earnestly with Herschel, the man who lived next door.

"How in the world can I feed my family, Guy?" Herschel was asking.

"A man can always make a garden," Daddy answered. "My family won't never starve. See that little hollow down there? I mean to clear it and grow my food." He gestured toward some bottom-land below the houses, a wild tangle of saplings, vines, and winter-dead underbrush. "Herschel, you could do that too."

"I don't know nothin' about makin' a garden," our neighbor responded helplessly. He hesitated. "But . . . if you could teach me and let me share, I'd do anything, Guy."

Daddy threw Herschel a quick, compassionate look that said he understood the man's fear, the near-begging, the pride reduced to dust. "Sure, Herschel," he said gently. "Reckon the Lord will help us both out."

As soon as the weather allowed, Daddy and Herschel cut saplings and took swingblades to the underbrush. They burned off dead weeds higher than my head, then broke up that land by hand. Even with a mule it would have been back-breaking work, yet neither man complained.

For weeks they worked every day except Sunday. Sunday was the Lord's day, and going to church and paying your tithe came as natural to Daddy as breathing. I asked him once, "When you only got ten dollars, how can you give a dollar to God? Doesn't He know how bad we need it?"

Daddy smiled. "Son, it's not my money to keep. That dollar belongs to Him." And he was firm about that, as firm as in his decision never to buy groceries on credit.

Spring comes early in mid-Georgia, and soon the men raked the ground, hot and sweaty work. They were excited now, and I could see that Herschel felt more hopeful.

One day they got hold of a little hand plow with a fourteen- or fifteen-inch wheel, one you could push. Using it took near superhuman effort, though. Tough and wiry as Daddy was, that stubborn ground needed more horsepower than the man possessed. That's when Herschel offered to pull the plow.

At first Daddy wouldn't hear of it. "Reckon I can make it, Herschel. Just take some time, that's all," he protested.

"Naw, Guy, let's figure how I can help you. I don't mind pullin'. Let's take these ropes . . ."

They rigged up a harness and Herschel hunched forward, the ropes biting into his chest and straining shoulders, and he pulled that plow like some powerful, sweating animal. Dad plowed straight as a die. At the end of the first row the men broke into grins.

"Now we'll change places," Daddy commanded.

"Naw, Guy, we're goin' good. I don't know nothing about plowin'. Let's just do it thisaway."

The Lord must have helped, because the garden came in good. Pole beans made a green tent I could play under, with ten- and twelve-inch-long beans dangling in thick clusters. All creation seemed to explode with food—corn, okra, butter beans, peas, cucumbers, tomatoes, cabbages, greens—overflowing with plenty for us and for Herschel's family, plus a mess to give away.

Mama taught Herschel's wife how to preserve. She turned our back porch into a canning center where the women put up jars of tomatoes, soup mix, beans, everything imaginable. Again, both families had plenty to share. Daddy gave God credit for the generous harvest. He offered his tithe, thanked God for everything, and believed himself rich.

Today, if I catch myself having doubts or hanging back when a job or a problem makes heavy demands on me, I summon up that picture of Daddy and Herschel toiling together, plowing with the humility of simple beasts on a long-ago spring afternoon. I ask myself, "Am I willing to put *my* back to the plow?"

Daddy and Herschel showed me how to plow deep and straight, without holding back. It works. And the crops come in abundantly.

Out on a Limb

Judi Frix

On a brittle winter afternoon in 1985 I walked along a row of bare trees on our peach farm, remembering how those trees had looked with their pink blossoms glowing on a spring morning. That sight was part of the dream my husband, L.G., and I had worked so hard for. It was a simple dream: to farm these acres of land and make a good country living for our six children. We'd worked at it for fourteen years. But now the dream was slipping away; L.G. had lost his battle with cancer, and the farm was in jeopardy.

The wind picked up, rattling the branches. I shivered. If only L.G. had had some insurance. If only I hadn't had to mortgage the farm after L.G. got sick. If only I had college training so I could get a good job. I sighed, unable to go on thinking of the future.

L.G. had grown up on a sharecropping farm, but had left his roots to find work in Atlanta. I was a city girl. After we married and our first baby was born, L.G. wanted to invest our savings in a farm—his lifetime dream. I wasn't exactly spilling over with enthusiasm. But as Ruth says in the Bible, "Whither thou goest, I will go" (Ruth 1:16). So at twenty-three, having never picked a tomato off a tomato plant, much less a peach off a tree, I followed L.G. out here to Talbotton from metro Atlanta to make a new life together.

The first years brought endless hours of work and small return. We barely scrimped through, surviving on venison, wild rabbit, and the previous summer's preserved fruits and vegetables. "L.G., this is pure craziness," I said to him time after time. "Why don't we sell out? There's no way to keep going."

But he didn't waver. "You gotta look to the future and have faith. That's all." That was L.G.'s simple farm-spun philosophy. I could only shake my head at it.

We planted more peach trees, many while I was carrying a child in me. "These trees will bear fruit," L.G. would say. "Nature feels the effort." We did make a go of it, and somehow, over the years, as our family and our orchards grew, L.G.'s dream became mine. He saw God in the land, and now I did too. I could feel Him in the touch of the soil on my fingertips.

Once, we had to sell off part of the land to survive. But survive we did, year after year, always striving for quality in our crops. Along with our peaches, we grew tomatoes and vegetables. We built a roadside farm stand to sell them, and customers came from miles away.

I thought my husband would always be clinging to the land along with me and the kids. Now he was dead, farm work was at a standstill, and our savings were gone. I had no idea what to do.

I turned and walked away from the orchard without looking back.

In the house, I huddled on the sofa with the kids—blonde Lathina, seventeen, a real mother's helper; merry Mary, thirteen, of the high spirits; dependable redheaded Jennifer, twelve; my little Molly, ten, blonde and energetic; Joshua, eight, L.G.'s special candidate for "Frix farmer of the future"; and Michael, four, a bundle of love. The house was full of quietness as they looked at me with unspoken questions. *What will happen now? Where will we go?* I had no answers to give them.

Long after they were asleep, I tossed in bed. Finally, as I lay beneath my warm quilt, I started to pray. "Lord, it's just me now," I said, my voice quivering. "I've got bills a mile high. But most important I have these six precious children to take care of. We love this place, these trees, this land. But, dear Lord, I don't see any way in the world I can hold on here. What am I going to do?"

I bit my lip, wanting to sob with grief and uncertainty. And suddenly I found myself thinking about L.G. and the years past and that stubborn faith of his that kept us pressing on no matter what. Every morning L.G. had slipped out of bed onto his knees to pray. He'd asked God for strength to do what had to be done, then he went out and did it.

There in the darkness my heart started to beat faster. Could it be that with simple, old-fashioned faith in God, the kids and I could run this place? Could I simply trust God to give me the strength and wisdom I needed, plain as that?

A mother and six children running a hundred-fifty-acre peach farm when farms were going under left and right—now there was a farfetched notion! It meant crawling out on a limb. But maybe that's what old-fashioned faith was about.

The next morning I told the children: "We're staying put. But we've got to hang together." Then I picked up the pruning shears and we headed out among our eight thousand trees.

In the weeks that followed, the kids and I rolled up our sleeves. I learned how to take a tractor's carburetor apart on the kitchen table and put it back together. I didn't even stop to think whether I could do such an outlandish thing. I worked hard—plowing, planting, mowing the orchard, and caring for the trees as if they were my own children. When the kids weren't in school they worked right along beside me, just as hard. What a team we were—Lathina doing the cooking; Mary driving the tractor to pull the wagon; Jennifer taking care of housework; Molly, Joshua, and Michael fetching and carrying.

For two years we lost nearly every peach to frost. To make up the losses, I hired myself out to do odd jobs. I wallpapered and painted houses. I did repairs and maintenance. I hired out as a cleaning woman and teacher's aide. Meanwhile, the children and I worked in the field, tending the trees.

Not a day went by that I didn't depend body and soul on God. He was always there, giving me that last bit of energy to finish the day, nudging me to keep on. Every time I lay down to rest, I prayed, "God, please give me the strength."

Spring came again and the trees burst into radiant blossoms. It was our make-it-or-break-it year. We started spraying early. We watched the fragile blooms grow into small, delicate peaches. Then, just as all prospects were looking good, I got up one morning to hear a news bulletin that the temperature would drop below freezing that night.

I sat at the kitchen table, despair growing in the pit of my stomach. All I could do was stir my coffee and wonder how we would go on. I couldn't help the question hammering in my mind. *Where are You, Lord?* One by one the children wandered in and gathered around the table. Little Michael slid his arms around my neck and squeezed with all the strength in his small body. Molly refilled my coffee cup. As I looked from one to the other, I noticed that despite the situation, there was no fear in their eyes. They seemed to trust that I would still provide, that Mama would be there for them no matter what. A smile tugged at my mouth. They were so right!

Sitting there with the new morning streaming through the window, I knew the same was true of God. Wasn't I His child, and wouldn't He be there for me no matter what? Adversity happened; that was part of the gamble of life. Surely God would no more desert me than I would desert one of my children.

"Let's do something about this!" I said to the kids.

I got on the phone and began to canvass friends, neighbors, and businesses for old tires. If we burned them at the edges of the orchards—and if the wind stayed strong—the smoke and warmth would fight the dangers of frost. By midafternoon, trucks were coming and going with tires—and people—to help. Then at 5:00 P.M. the wind slowed down. The weather bureau warned of a still, clear night. The fires wouldn't help unless we had a helicopter to stir the air.

Frantically I called every helicopter service I could find. None was left to be hired. We lighted the fires anyway. Near midnight, when stars twinkled overhead and bitter cold had begun to creep deep into the orchards, a call came. Someone had found a helicopter and pilot.

Four nights we burned tires—running from one location to another, refueling and feeding the flames. On two of those four nights the helicopter flew back and forth, churning the air. The fifth day broke with warmer weather.

After everyone left, I walked through the orchards. Smoke still hovered in the trees. I pinched bud after bud for a sign of life. There was no way to be sure.

At home I opened the door and found, sound asleep, sprawled in every direction, my six smutty children and a dozen neighbors and friends. We had done our best. It was in God's hands now.

And come May, you should have seen the fruit God grew on those trees—big Georgia peaches, their plump cheeks covered with pink fuzz. What a truly beautiful sight to behold!

Day after day the kids and I picked and packed peaches till nightfall. As they climbed into bed, I drove the peaches ninety miles to the market in Atlanta, getting back home around 3:00 A.M., time for a couple hours' sleep before the day started again. There was only One who could have given me such stamina. When the last peach was picked, I lifted my eyes into a smiling blue sky and thanked God.

Today I've almost paid off the medical bills and I'm working on the mortgage. I don't know if we'll be here on this land forever. But I do know that the kids have experienced for themselves the goodness of working together on God's earth. They've learned that the long hours of physical work, when you push your body to perform, make for better athletes and cheerleaders, and that the same physical work is a home cure for depression. Having farm responsibilities has helped the six of them become achievers and award-winners in their schoolwork and scouting and 4-H activities.

Best of all, like their father and me, the kids have seen God in the land. They've seen that faith is believing and hoping in God in good times *and* bad, trusting Him to be there with the strength and help you need—*if only you don't give up.*

Our kids . . . they're a dream come true. A bumper crop of real Georgia peaches.

The Migrant ?❧

Diana Coe

It all began one hot June day last summer. A doctor stuck his head into the department of the Memphis charity hospital where I worked as a candy-striper and asked if anyone could speak Spanish. I meekly admitted that I did.

The doctor then grabbed my arm and led me to the fifth floor where his non-English-speaking patient lay. My first glimpse of this man filled me with pity and horror; one of his legs was amputated below the knee. I gulped hard, then introduced myself to Luis Hernández, little knowing that the humble thirty-four-year-old Mexican migrant would play an important role in strengthening my faith in God.

After three hours of conversation, I became deeply interested in Luis. Two weeks before, after his corn crop failed, Luis had illegally crossed the Mexican border to earn enough money to feed his wife and four young children. Unable to find a job in Texas, Luis had decided to move on to Florida where Spanish is spoken by many of the residents. By hitching rides on freight trains, he had arrived in Memphis.

It was there that the accident happened. Running alongside the moving boxcar, he had grabbed for the handhold. However, because he had not eaten in eight days and was weak, Luis fell. The train crushed his leg. When I met him, he was alone in a hospital in a foreign country; he could speak no English; one of his legs was gone; and he had lost his faith in God.

Driving home, I thought about Luis. What was his future? He earned three hundred dollars a year and lived in a one-room shack with a dirt floor and no electricity or plumbing. I knew that in Mexico there was no welfare system to take care of him.

That night I turned to God and prayed as I had never prayed before, asking Him to guide me in helping this man.

The next day I gave Luis some stationery, and he began to write to his wife about his accident. As he wrote, tears of overwhelming grief streamed down his face. While sitting at his bedside, I suddenly knew how I could help him. I would get Luis an artificial leg!

That afternoon I went to the hospital's physical therapy department and excitedly told the therapists my idea. Giving many valid arguments, they all said it was impossible. First, Luis would be ineligible for welfare because he was an alien, and an artificial leg would cost about five hundred dollars. Second, I would not have enough time to order the leg because as soon as he recovered, Luis would be deported. Third, I did not have a place where Luis could stay for two months while his stump healed. Finally, they reasoned, if I was found helping him, I would be charged with aiding a criminal.

Completely convinced that my plan was indeed impossible, I went home and cried myself to sleep. However, the next morning, instead of simply crying about the situation, I prayed. I asked God to guide me in helping Luis.

After praying, I felt assured that Luis would get the leg. Although I didn't know how he'd get it, I knew he would. From that moment on, my faith never wavered. No matter how impossible the situation appeared, I knew that God would help me overcome it.

For the next month I visited Luis every day and made contacts for money. Each of the clubs and churches that I went to turned me down because they had "other charity projects." After each refusal, all the therapists, my family, and even Luis told me to give up.

Yet I kept praying, knowing that God would let Luis get that artificial leg. Two weeks passed without any response from my contacts. Then one day when I arrived at the hospital I found a minister with Luis. The minister listened intently while I told him about my idea for the artificial leg. A week later he gave us our first contribution—a hundred dollars that his church had raised.

The same week, several other churches that I had previously contacted began to contribute money, fruit baskets, and Spanish Bibles. By the end of that week, I had collected four hundred dollars. Clutching this money, I went to a prosthesis shop in Memphis and told my story. Before knowing how much money I had collected, the owner of the shop offered me the artificial leg for three hundred seventy-five dollars—a reduction of more than a hundred dollars.

After that eventful week, Luis's faith in God became very real. His whole outlook on life changed. His eyes changed from those of a scared, nervous animal to those of a confident, trusting person at peace with himself and God. He no longer had trouble sleeping or contemplated suicide.

The day that Luis had to leave the hospital finally arrived.

Although I didn't have a place for him to stay, Luis and I both knew that God would provide one. While checking Luis out of the hospital, a social worker informed me of a boardinghouse that cost seventy-five dollars a month. I called the landlady of this house and, knowing that God would somehow furnish the money for the rent, I asked her to hold the room for two days.

That night Luis stayed at our house. While we were eating, the president of a church youth group called to contribute exactly seventy-five dollars. God *had* provided the money for the rent!

Luis's stump healed beautifully and the big day became a reality. I will never forget that exciting moment in the doctor's office when Luis stood on his artificial leg for the first time and stared into the mirror. Then, without uttering a word, we looked at each other and with tears rolling down our cheeks, we lowered our heads and thanked God for "the impossible."

The Story Behind the Story   *Van Varner*

Luis's illegal entry was the single greatest barrier Diana had to hurdle in her campaign for him. For Diana the decision to help the Mexican was a decision of the heart. She was convinced that unless she did something for him—and there was no one else to do it—he would have to go home without a leg, without hope, and with the threat that he and his family might starve.

Once Diana made her brave decision, she pursued it relentlessly, driving fifty miles a day back and forth to the John Gaston Hospital, giving up a summer vacation trip she had been looking forward to, speaking before group after group seeking donations. But most charitable groups were afraid to help because of the legal complications, so Diana went to see a lawyer from the congregation of her Methodist church in Collierville.

John Porter, the attorney she consulted, simply could not see how anybody or any group, especially a church group, could ever be prosecuted for helping a human being in desperate need. "If they put you in jail, honey," he said, "they'll have to put me in with you."

That was the encouragement that broke the jam, and by October Luis went home with his new limb. The next January, Luis wrote that at last he had a job—driving a tractor!

Our Blue-Eyed Maverick

Nelson Pendergrass

It was early December—breeding season on our ranch in eastern Oklahoma. We had two hundred heifers to move, separate by breed, and put into pastures with the bulls. My two sons and I saddled our horses and swung up on their backs with that pleasant squeaking of leather on leather.

My twelve-year-old, Terry, was riding Big Man, a large bay who had months of training as a cow horse and could do more than his share of work. My nine-year-old, Buddy, was riding his App, another experienced horse. I rode the dun mare. Though she was green at working cattle, she too could help if I handled her properly.

As we rode along, driving the heifers in front of us, our bodies swayed in that comfortable rolling motion that always makes me feel at peace with God and man. The faint odor of hickory smoke drifted on the crisp fall breeze from our neighbors' house over the ridge. *It's a beautiful day,* I thought. *It's filled with the kind of rugged beauty any cowboy would love.* But my mind was troubled. I was thinking of the boy who had been living with us for the past year.

David was a nice-looking sixteen-year-old kid with blue eyes and light brown hair. He was taller and bigger than my boys, and he should have been with us now. But he couldn't be counted on when it came to doing important jobs. I had sent him to pick pecans with my wife.

David was a delinquent boy from a broken home. I had taken custody of him from the juvenile court, thinking that a good Christian home would be the kind of environment that could change a boy like David. I thought I was the kind of man that could help him change.

But David was a different breed. He had no self-respect and whenever he was put under any pressure to do a better job, he was ready to quit. The summer before, I got him a job with an electronics repair shop in Bixby. He started out by doing fine work, and his employer gave him more responsibility. But when his boss sent him on errands in his pickup, David would drive like a maniac. When his boss told him to cut out the recklessness, David stormed home.

"He can't talk to me like that!" David told me that evening. "I'm not working for him anymore."

"You can't quit just because your boss corrects you for what you've done wrong," I said. I'd grown up during the Depression, and to me work was honorable wherever it was found. "You can't just throw away a good job. Life doesn't work that way. With that attitude you're always going to have trouble."

"I don't care what happens to me. Just leave me alone!" he said, stomping away.

Months had now passed and I had run out of answers for David's problems. *Maybe I should send him back,* I thought. But part of me knew I'd try to keep him until he was out of high school. Then he'd be on his own, and it would be a relief to see that sullen boy go. He was simply the kind of kid I couldn't help. What more could the Lord expect me to do?

Buddy opened the gate and we started herding the heifers into the pasture. To a working cowboy, nothing compares to the feel of a strong horse beneath you as you move into a herd of cattle. But today the confidence I usually felt when riding Big Man was missing. The dun, I could sense, didn't know what she was about.

And this part of the job took special skill. The corral gate was alongside an oil-and-chat road with wide, grassy shoulders. It was always a scramble to turn the cattle in the right direction and into the corral—and sure enough, about twenty of the heifers headed out the wrong way.

I tackled the job of driving them back to the main herd. I eased my mare through the twenty and closed in on the lead heifer, a black whiteface. The dun mare, seeming to know she was supposed to stop the heifer, broke into a gallop. Suddenly the heifer swung her head to the right and lurched across our path! My horse reared. *We fell. Hard.*

When I opened my eyes neither the dun mare nor the heifer was in sight. I was lying on the grassy shoulder of the oil-and-chat road with the short clipped Bermuda grass pricking my cheek.

Through blurry eyes I saw the face of my older son.

"Daddy?" he screamed. Tears streaked his cheeks. "Daddy?"

I didn't know what he was seeing, but I knew it couldn't be good. "I'll be all right, son," I said, even though I knew something was terribly wrong. "Ride home and tell your mother to call an ambulance." He hesitated only a moment. Then Big Man's hooves thundered and he was gone.

I couldn't move my right arm, I had a burning pain in my right leg, and my left arm between elbow and hand was bent grotesquely at a right angle. I wasn't in pain—but I knew that would come later.

The ambulance screamed its way over the country roads to Tulsa, rushing me to St. Francis Hospital. Once I was inside the emergency room, a team of doctors went to work mending my crushed body.

After long hours in surgery with one of Tulsa's finest orthopedic surgeons, I awoke in the intensive-care unit. Casts encased my elevated arms and one leg. It would be a long time before I would ride a horse again.

As I lay in bed, I thought that now I wasn't physically able to deal with a delinquent boy, David would probably have to go. In fact, I kind of liked the idea of having our home to ourselves, without a stubborn outsider to take care of. I'd see what would happen once I got home.

On the third day in intensive care, sudden, searing pain tore through my chest. A signal from one of my monitoring machines brought a nurse on the run. A blood clot was passing through my heart. The pain was unbearable. For the first time in my life, I wanted to die.

I gasped for air. But it hurt too much to breathe. *Better to just drift away,* I told myself. *Away from the fear, from the pain. Forever.*

But there was the nurse, her face not six inches from mine.

"Breathe. You've got to *breathe,*" she said.

Leave me alone, I wanted to scream. *Let me die.*

But no, she was still there.

"Breathe," she said. "Breathe . . . Breathe . . . *Breathe.*" I was willing to give up, but she was not. Again and again, I fought to take a breath as she called to me.

The surgeon and heart specialist appeared. But even as they worked, the nurse remained my lifeline. As long as she wouldn't give up, I couldn't either. I *had* to go on. *Breathe,* she said. I did.

The crisis passed somewhere in the middle of the night. I made it through.

As weeks passed, my body mended and I finally left the hospital. I went home with the idea that I'd have to send David away. I didn't think I would be strong enough to put up with a boy who refused to cooperate.

Then one morning when I awoke I discovered that David and my pickup were gone. He had roared off the night before without a word—and it now seemed clear he wasn't coming back. It made me sick and angry at the same time. After all we had done for the boy, how could he treat us like that? As far as I was concerned that was the last straw. *Let the juvenile court deal with this,* I thought. *He's hopeless.*

Before the day was over I had a call from the sheriff's office in Russellville, Arkansas. They had David and my stolen pickup. We went to get him the next day. As I followed the jailer, the jingle of his keys echoed in the little block of cells.

"You've got company," the jailer said.

David glanced up at me through the bars, sneered, and looked away.

"David, don't you realize how serious this all is?" I asked.

"I don't care," he said. "Just go away! Leave me alone!"

In an instant his words brought it all back to me—the pain of the blood clot, my wish that the nurse would go away and leave me alone. I stared at David. This boy was in pain. But the nurse had not given up on me. "Breathe! Breathe!" she had said. "Don't quit." That nurse hadn't quit on me—but here I was about to quit on David. Suddenly I saw myself as an easygoing church man who was ready to give up when the job the Lord gave him got a little hard.

I thought of my horses. The mare that threw me had only done so because she lacked training. I hadn't sent *her* away.

I thought of the nurse who had understood what I was going through. If it hadn't been for her understanding, I wouldn't be standing where I was now, ready to pass judgment on David.

Then I understood what *I* had to do.

"David, as long as you're under my supervision, you're *not* giving up on life." My voice grew firmer as I spoke. "And I'm not giving up on you either. We're *not* quitting. You're coming home. And you and I and the Lord are going to get through all of this."

The sneer left his face and his eyes widened in surprise. "Okay," he said quietly. I turned and strode down the echoing hall out of the cell block.

As the months passed, working with David was not easy, but I was determined that if he couldn't make it on his own, I would be his lifeline. I would pray for him, talk to him, discipline him, and love him whether he liked it or not. *Breathe,* I seemed to be saying to him. *Breathe, David!*

Little by little he became less stubborn and more cooperative. When finally he came of age and moved away, it was like seeing one of our own sons leaving.

David has been gone for many years now. But he writes every so often. He's married and has two kids that he's just crazy about. He's been on the same job for over six years.

David brought his family by to visit the other day. After he ushered his wife and kids out of the car, he came up to me in the yard where I was standing under an old oak. His eyes were twinkling, his hair was neatly trimmed, and he had a big smile on his face. I raised my arm for a handshake, but surprisingly, he pushed my hand aside, slipped his arms around me, and gave me a big hug. "Thanks, Nelson," he said.

Even a cowboy has a pretty hard time keeping his eyes dry at a time like that.

Reaching for the Light 🦢

Brian Barber

We farm on the South Dakota prairie. Our land is gently rolling, marked by cedar draws and rimmed to the north by the Cheyenne River. Our work is unending, with crops to nurture and cattle to tend.

A few years back, when I first farmed on my own, I felt I didn't have time for anything else, even though my wife, Andrea, and I had vowed to give more time to God. I was just too buried in my chores. The Lord's work would have to wait until farming took less time.

Until farming took less time. Now there's a comical thought. Farming will forever mean working the same hours as the sun, and those are *all* hours of the day. And so, even though my excuse sounded good, I knew I shouldn't live by it. In its shadow my whole life could go by and I'd never get to know God well. And yet, what could I do? I *did* work all hours of the day. Can a bone-tired man really grow in his faith?

Well, I eventually learned the answer to that question, and I have my land to thank. My land—God's earth—taught me how to grow.

My lesson came in 1979, a year western South Dakota land

suffered greatly. The winter was cold and snowless, causing the winter wheat crop to freeze and die. In May I hoped to put in spring wheat, but after the snowless winter and a rainless April, the fields were too drought-stricken for wheat.

Needing hardy crops that didn't require much water, I put half my crop acreage in barley, oats, and Sudan grass—a forage crop. A seed salesman then told me that I ought to put the other half in sunflowers.

Sunflowers? I'd never seen a sunflower grow anywhere but in a kitchen garden or along the roadside. Nonetheless, they were said to be pretty hardy and marketable for their oil. They were worth a try.

For a week I poured sunflower seed into the parched soil. The days were hot and cloudless. At day's end, dust in my teeth, I'd kneel in the field and take the earth in my hand. It was heated and dry, like beach sand under a noonday sun.

A couple of weeks passed, and hardly any seedlings came up. At last, on June 15th, clouds came along and rain began to fall. We soon saw, though, that this wasn't the long, gentle rain we needed. Instead we got cloudbursts that the soil couldn't soak up fast enough.

Four days later, when the sun came out, the topsoil was still wet and greasy, and when wet topsoil bakes under a hot sun, it turns crusty. Really *hard* and crusty, like burned bread. The sunflower seedlings were now trapped underground.

I was too disheartened to do anything, my one true cash crop— *buried.* A few days later I decided to go one last time to the sunflower field.

And there I saw an amazing thing—sunflower shoots everywhere! At first I was pretty baffled; the ground was still crusty, too hard for any seedling to push through. But then I saw that the seedlings hadn't sprouted in straight lines. Instead of pushing straight up, as they would have done in loose soil, they wandered underground until they found cracks in the hardpan. *Then* they pushed up and broke into the light.

Later, I returned to the field with Andrea and our two children, Janet and Shane and I showed them the sprouts. "There's some incredible determination in every sunflower seed . . . some power that enables them to seek the sun and the air no matter what," I pointed out.

As the days went by, and as the sunflowers grew, I continued to think about their growing power. This power *to grow no matter what.* The sunflowers had within their seeds an indomitable strength that enabled them to reach for the sun. Did I have, deep within me, a similar strength that would enable me to reach for God? A strength that could help me overcome the long hours and unending worries of farm life? . . .

Over the next few months I tried to answer this question. The harvest arrived and with it came even longer hours. But that field of golden sunflowers—once buried, but now so tall—told me that I needn't feel buried by weariness. There *were* ways of riding above the drudgery—ways that led to God.

As I drove the combine down the somewhat crooked rows, I'd carry lines of Scripture with me, verses telling of long-ago harvests, and, mulling them over, I'd feel connected to the farmers of the Bible. Feeling this connection, I was less bothered by the work's monotony. Instead, I saw myself taking part in one of God's greatest blessings: the bountiful harvest.

And, at the very start of the day, with my family at the breakfast table, I'd read from God's Word. Our quiet fellowship was a comfort to me as I went off to work with the roaring machines. Once again I felt less weary and more blessed by God.

These weren't big things we did, but eventually they assured me that the sunflowers and I did have a certain strength in common. The strength to reach for God's rejuvenating light. The strength to grow, no matter what.

Faith Holds On in the Darkness

Give Me a Strong Heart

Viola Jacobson Berg

Dear Father,
give me a strong heart
that will not wither away
in puny faith.
But may each delay,
each disappointment,
each closed door
be a signal
to hold on more tightly,
to pray more fervently,
to trust more completely,
confident that when the answer comes,
it will be right.

The Geese and I

H. Ramsey Terhune

It was a thrilling sight. Our flock of domestic gray geese were winging in for the night feeding, and the majestic grace of their flight was uplifting, stirring. Once again, winter had dropped a cold, cheerless blanket on the pastureland. All natural feeding areas had been choked off. For survival, the geese again depended upon their human providers.

For years, the providers had been my wife, Frannie, and me. Frannie loved watching the regal arrival. It was almost something spiritual for her. Even when she became too ill for the cold outdoors, she would go to a window and watch.

Last New Year's Day I was once more out in the snow-covered fields, calling my searching cry. "Hey, boys! Come, boys!" Their familiar response came from somewhere on the farm.

On they flew. Some were at chest height, some above my head, all of them dropping their legs to break their speed and land at my feet. Now we were all waiting respectfully for the old gander. No one ever stirred or ate until he arrived. There was a reason.

On a windy day the previous October, a stray bird dog had savagely charged into the flock. In a wild flurry, the terrified geese had all scrambled or flown to safety—all, that is, except the old gander. A leader does not run. Undaunted, he lowered his head and spread his wings to meet the challenge. Standing his ground, he hissed at the predator that threatened to destroy his wards.

The battle raged for just a few moments, the gander beating off the dog with blows from his powerful wings. But in the fight, one of those wings was broken. Quietly the old bird slipped into the farm pond, there to remain alone for three weeks until nature's healing hand restored him to his position of leadership in the flock.

That New Year's Day I watched the injured gander respond to the feed call. He could not fly, but he used his good wing to hop across the snow to where his followers patiently awaited him.

As I watched, an odd thought struck me. We were both cripples, the gander and I. He was grounded by an injury. I was grounded by grief. Back in May, my precious Frannie went home to Heaven after a two-year struggle with cancer. Seven months later, I was still sorrow-bound. How could I ever fly again? My hurt was too paralyzing.

But now the old gander's struggling approach was flashing a clear message. Yes, fate had been cruel to him, but with determination and instinct *he* was carrying on. I, though blessed in faith and intelligence, was helpless because I had been unwilling to be reconciled to the perfect will of Providence. And the firm foundation laid by His sustaining Word was all but ignored.

Suddenly, by observing the gander, the full light of conviction shone on me. Quickly a lifting was granted on the wings of penitent prayer. I was upward-bound far above the deep abyss of sorrow. And I could hear the feed call, "Come unto Me. Come unto Me."

Clear and strong I was hearing *my* Provider. And I was obeying—I would fly again.

The Secret of Our Survival

James E. Ray

"Pssst."

I struggled upright on the damp pallet in my solitary cell to hear better. It had sounded like a whisper.

No, I must have been hallucinating. I slumped back, wondering how long it had been since my 105 Thunderchief had been shot down as we bombed a railroad bridge on the Hanoi-China supply line.

That was May 8, 1966. I tried to forget the weeks since, the endless interrogations, the torture that left me screaming in agony.

Now I wished I had gone down with the plane. Anything would be better than the desolation, the awful sense of guilt at writing a confession under torture, the aloneness.

There! I heard it again. Now an unmistakable, "Hey, buddy?"

I scrambled flat on the floor and peered through the crack under the door. I could see I was in one of many cells facing a narrow, walled courtyard. The whisper had come from the next cell. I whispered back. He introduced himself as Bob Purcell, another Air Force man. We waited as the guard passed and then began to converse.

Soon all the prisoners on that yard were secretly whispering.

We started by learning about each other, where we were from, our families. One day I asked Bob what church he went to.

"Catholic," he said. "And you?"

"Baptist."

Bob was quiet for a moment, as if my mention of church evoked deep memories. Then he asked, "Do you know any Bible verses?"

"Well, the Lord's Prayer," I answered.

"Everyone knows that."

"How about the Twenty-third Psalm?"

"Only a little."

I began whispering it. He'd repeat each line after me. A little later he whispered the entire Psalm back to me.

Other prisoners joined in, sharing verses they knew. Through these contacts a fellowship grew among us. The others said that I shouldn't feel bad about "confessing" under torture. "We've all done it," they assured me. I didn't feel so alone anymore.

As the number of prisoners grew, two of us shared a cell. My first roommate was Larry Chesley, a Mormon from Idaho. Though we had a few differences of belief, our common denominators were the Bible and Jesus Christ, and we were able to share and write down a great deal of Scripture.

For by now it had become vital to our daily existence. Often racked with dysentery, weakened by the diet of rice and thin cabbage and pumpkin soup, our physical lives had shrunk within the prison walls. We spent twenty hours a day locked in our cells. And those Bible verses became rays of light, constant assurances of His love and care.

We made ink from brick dust and water or drops of medicine. We'd write verses on bits of toilet paper and pass them on to others, dropping them behind a loose brick at the toilets.

It was dangerous to pass these on. Communication between cells was forbidden and a man unlucky enough to be caught passing a note would be forced to stand with his arms up against a wall for several days, without sleep.

But the urge to share developed inventiveness. One night I lay with my ear pressed against the rough wooden wall of my cell to hear *Thump . . . thumpety thump* as somewhere on the wall, cells away, a fellow POW tapped out in Morse code: "I will lift up my eyes unto the hills, from whence cometh my help" (Psalm 121:1).

He tapped out his name—Russ Temperly—and passed on the seven other verses in that Psalm which I scratched on the concrete floor with a piece of broken tile. "My help cometh from the Lord," the Psalm assured us, and with that assurance came God's Presence, soothing us, telling us to fear not.

By 1968, more of us were squeezed together and for two years four of us lived in an eight-by-eight-foot cell. In this close proximity, even minor personality rubs could flare into violent explosions. For instance, one guy liked to whistle. Talk about getting on your nerves! Some of the verses that helped us bear with one another were from Romans: "Every man among you is not to think of himself more highly than he ought to think . . ." (12:3, 5).

Only by following Christ's teachings in constant forgiveness, patience, and understanding were we able to get along together. The whistler? We recommended a schedule for when he should whistle.

Two and a half years went by before I could write Dad and Mother. A year later I was allowed to receive my first letter. In the meantime we subsisted on letters written two thousand years ago.

By late 1970, almost all of the American POWs had been moved to Ha Lo, the main prison in downtown Hanoi. Newspapers later called this the Hanoi Hilton; we called it Heartbreak Hotel.

Some fifty of us lived, ate, and slept together in one large room. Thanksgiving came shortly after we moved in and we held a brief service. We all were surprised to find how many of the men knew Scripture, learned from those verses passed along in whispers, bits of paper, and wall thumpings. We immediately made plans for a Christmas service. A committee was formed and started to work.

Bits of green and red thread decorated the walls, a piece of green cloth was draped like a tree. Our crèche was made of figures carved from soap rations or molded from papier-mâché of moistened toilet paper.

We pooled the verses we knew and we now had a "consensus Bible," written covertly on bits of paper, some of it King James, some Phillips, some Revised Standard. But it served. It was the only Bible we had. As we sat in silence, the reader began: "In those days a decree went out from Caesar Augustus that all the world should be enrolled . . ." As he completed this verse, a six-man choir sang "O Little Town of Bethlehem."

He went on: "And she gave birth to her first born son and wrapped him in swaddling clothes . . ." "Away in the manger no crib for His bed, Our Little Lord Jesus lay down His sweet head," sang the choir.

Once again I was a youngster in Sunday school at the First

Baptist Church. Time had rolled back for all of us grizzled men in prison pajamas as, with eyes shining and tears trickling through beards, we joined in the singing. Glinting in the light from the kerosene lamp was a cross made of silver foil.

Occasionally the guards would knock on the door, ordering us not to sing, but they finally gave up. Our program continued into a communion service led by Air Force Lt. Tom Moe. A Lutheran, he sang his church's communion chants as Episcopalians, Methodists, and men of other denominations bowed their heads together.

A Jewish prisoner told us about the Hanukkah tradition and entertained us by singing, "the eight days of Hanukkah" to the tune of "The Twelve Days of Christmas." Amid the laughing and singing, we looked up to find the prison camp commander and his English-speaking interrogators watching.

Later that night, after many months of our asking, the commander brought us a real Bible, the first any of us had seen in prison. He said we could keep it for one hour. We made the best of it. One of us read aloud the favorite passages called out by the others. We also checked some of our handwritten scripture. Amazingly, we weren't very far off.

We didn't see that little cloth-bound King James version again for several months. Finally, after continual requests, one of us was allowed to go out and copy from it for "one hour" each week.

But when we'd start to copy, the interrogator would plant his elbow on the Bible for the first fifteen minutes. Then, after he'd let us start, he'd ask mundane questions to distract us. I'd just ignore him and write as fast as I could. The next week we'd have to return the previous week's copy work. They seemed to be afraid for us to keep the Scriptures, as if they sensed the spiritual help kept us from breaking.

From that we learned a most important lesson. Bible verses on paper aren't one iota as useful as Scriptures burned into your mind where you can draw on them for guidance and comfort.

After five weeks we didn't see the Bible again. But that had been enough time for us to memorize collectively the Sermon on the Mount, Romans 12, First Corinthians 13, and many of the Psalms. Now we had our own "living Bible," walking around the room. By this time, too, we held Sunday worship services and Sunday school classes. Some of the "eat, drink, and be merry" type fighter pilots took part, some of them contributing as much to the services as the guys who had always professed to be Christians.

We learned to rise above our surroundings, to overcome the

material with the spiritual. In constantly exercising our minds, we developed teaching seminars in which we studied special subjects led by men experienced in various fields. These included learning Spanish, French, German, Russian. I particularly enjoy music and will never forget the music course.

Bill Butler, the leader of this program, drew a giant-sized piano keyboard on the floor with brick dust. Then, standing on a "key," one assistant would hum its note. Other assistants, up the keyboard, hummed each note of the chord that was being demonstrated, while Bill explained how chord progression works.

Two years passed this way at Heartbreak Hotel, years of continuing degradation, sickness, endless hunger, and never knowing whether we'd ever see home again. But instead of going mad or becoming animals, we continued to grow as a community of men, sustaining one another in compassion and understanding.

For as one of the verses I heard thumped out on the wall one night said: "Man does not live by bread alone, but by every word that proceeds out of the mouth of the Lord" (Deuteronomy 8:3).

His Word became our rock.

Our Time of Testing

Stacey Harrison

The results of the vote were read by the secretary of the church board. Looking immediately at my mom, I saw her head drop to her chest. I remember a lot of ringing in my ears after the announcement, and to this day I don't remember how I got from my pew to the parsonage. I only remember my parents standing at the back of the sanctuary, shaking hands and smiling as they had done every Sunday for over six years. We were voted out, or as Dad put it, "We just didn't get enough votes to stay." Out—by only three votes.

At the parsonage, my sister and two brothers and I sat at the dining room table waiting . . . waiting . . . it seemed like an eternity before my parents came in. We kids searched their faces for a clue as to what our future would hold now. First, we just looked at each other in shock and disbelief. Then, Mom put her face in her hands and cried.

After the vote, we had been told that we had to be out of the parsonage in three months. Mom and Dad began sending résumés out across the districts in our denomination, but there just didn't seem to be any place for us to serve. The board members did allow us to stay in the parsonage three months longer.

I had always loved and feared God. It was the way I was taught in our family. We are very close and really do enjoy being with each other. Many times I had seen my parents call on the sick, comfort the bereaved, and leave us in order to carry out their pastoral duties. I just could not understand how these same people could vote against my father. When they needed him, he was there. When they were out of work, he was there. How could a loving God allow this to happen to us? I started blaming God. I got very angry at Him.

The whole school knew about our situation. Everybody knows everything in a small town like Apple Valley. My senior year, my last year at high school, was coming up in the autumn. It was to be my greatest year. All of a sudden my whole world seemed to be falling to pieces. I decided that I hated school, church, people, and God. I decided to live my life all by myself, not really trusting anyone.

June came and we still had no assignment. Some members of the church were going on a trip and told my parents we could live in their mobile home. With only two bedrooms, it was rather uncomfortable for a family of six. Fortunately, Mom had a job, but she came home from work tired and depressed. Dad spent the entire day looking for work. Weekends he'd travel miles to preach at one of the churches in our district.

Never once did I hear my father blame anyone for our circumstances. He never changed in his attitude toward people or God. I would tell him, "Dad, you were the one who built the new eighty thousand dollar parsonage for less than half that much. You did so much of the work yourself. You were the one who organized and remodeled the old church building. You were the one who helped the church raise the money and pay the bills . . . you . . . " and I would always end up crying and getting mad at him.

Even when he finally got some construction work and started a grading business on the side, I was angry at him because he graded the property for the new house for the associate minister the church had called. I felt that the people there had no right asking my father to do something for them for free when they had done what they'd done to him. How could my father be so good? Especially when his daughter would rather have blown up the church than see it prosper.

We were barely making it on Mom's salary and things were not getting much better, so when school was out my older sister went to live with some friends from the church and I went to stay with my Grandfather Smith. He is the neatest grandfather in the whole world. He was a boy-preacher from Osage, Oklahoma, and preached for over forty years. During my stay, he taught me many things.

Most of all, he talked about my attitude. He said that God knows what we go through and how it hurts, but He is more concerned about our attitudes. Our attitudes will either make or break us. If we didn't have the valleys and the trials then there would be no victories. No obstacles to work through. No life. No action. Grandfather made me see that my own father could love and hold no grudges because of Jesus Christ.

My grandfather really made me start changing my thoughts about people and things. He made me see that God didn't hate my father. Rather, He loved him and was teaching him things that would be a blessing to him and others later on.

During the months I was with Grandfather, I noticed he was losing weight and getting paler. Grandmother finally got him to see a doctor. The news was bad. He had inoperable and incurable cancer of the blood and bone marrow. I had to return home to my parents. A builder had let my parents rent one of his homes at half-price until we could find a house.

Grandfather was given four days to live. Again, I watched my parents closely. Never once did they panic. Oh, how I wished I could have that kind of control and confidence. Dad would always say, "Stacey, when you are going through the hard places and it looks as though you have been given a bad deal, remember . . . there is always someone out there hurting more than you are."

It was amazing how God looked after us. When Mom didn't have the gas money to drive to see Grandfather, or we didn't know where the money would come from to pay for groceries, God would use someone to supply our needs. Dad's car quit running, and one of the members of the church found out and fixed it for free. Help was always sent just before it was too late. I had never seen this happen before.

Uncle Carl, who isn't even a Christian, called Mom and asked her if she believed what she had heard preached all her life. Mom said she did. Uncle Carl said, "Okay, I'm calling for the elders of the church to lay hands on Dad for his healing." Within twenty-four hours, over forty people had gathered in that hospital room in Northridge, California. They sang songs, prayed, and had the faith to believe that my grandfather could be healed. That same night he sat up and even walked down the hospital corridor, looking for something to eat. The following Sunday, he was released from the hospital, the cancer in remission and his blood normal.

That day the entire family sat at Grandfather's feet and listened to one of the greatest sermons I have ever heard. As I sat and looked into my parents' faces, so serene and trusting, I thought: *Even if I never have a home of my own or any sort of material wealth, I am really blessed.* Being with my family and knowing that I am loved by God makes me wealthy indeed. I wouldn't trade my experiences with anyone. They are mine to keep, to remember, and to learn from. I can learn to forgive and to keep going even when I don't feel like it.

This past year, my senior year, has been one of the greatest years of my life. I have learned something that isn't taught in textbooks. I have seen faith work. My attitude has become new. I know that I will face many more problems ahead, but now I have some real experiences to look back on and remember. "If thou canst believe, all things are possible" (Mark 9:23).

My parents are still without a church assignment. Our house is gone, our regular income is gone, our security in terms of material things is gone. But we are a family united and confident in God's Word and His truth. We are ready for the future, wherever He leads.

What a Year That Was!   *Van Varner*

What a jigsaw-puzzle of a year for the Harrison family—all its pieces thrown into upheaval and disarray. Stacey's father lost his pastorate; Stacey's grandfather lost his health; and Stacey herself lost her faith. But by the time I arrived in Apple Valley to interview Stacey, the pieces were being sorted out and a picture was forming.

Apple Valley lies in the high desert country of southern California. It's a place of long, empty vistas, of ancient Joshua trees standing lonely and freakish on the landscape, and in January, when I was there, it was a place of biting wind—blowing cold. In the Harrison home, however, there was nothing but warmth. I don't know why I expected to find a dour family, maybe because the events in Stacey's story were all so dark, but this family was lively and fun, and everybody in it, especially Stacey's parents, Don and Patty, seemed young.

Stacey's older sister, Kim, was away at college but her two younger brothers, Ron and Tim, were on hand and, in a surprise visit, so were the grandparents of Stacey's story, Floyd and Ruth Smith. With all the cast of characters neatly assembled, it was easy for me to get my own picture of what had been happening to them. And these are some of the things I learned:

Yes, it was a hard time for every single member of the Harrison family. It was also a time of testing. In the Church of the Nazarene, as in some other Protestant denominations, the pastor is reviewed and voted on by the congregation periodically; being voted out is not really a rare occurrence. Still, the vote took the Reverend Donald O. Harrison by surprise—perhaps he'd been moving too vigorously for his congregation; he's still not sure of the reasons why—but during that year, both he and his wife, Patty, put their faith to the test by accepting their setback with grace, with no ill will toward those who voted against them, and with hard work. The boys, Ron and Tim, worked hard, too, mowing lawns, doing landscape work to bring in much-needed money.

Stacey, however, reacted differently. She put her faith to the test by doubting God, by questioning Him; and God answered in an extraordinary way. Because of the struggles at home, Stacey was sent to spend the summer months with her grandparents in Northridge, California. The timing couldn't have been more precise. As Stacey drew closer to these wise, older people, her grandfather, who'd spent his life serving God, supplied the answers that his hurting and doubting granddaughter needed. Meanwhile, as Grandfather Smith grew increasingly thin and weak from the "incurable" cancer—the doctors expected him to die—Stacey was at his side, buoying *his* spirits, giving her grandmother the very help and support *she* now needed so badly. And just to add one last piece to this incredible mosaic, everyone in the family, all of them, put their faith on the line in Grandfather Smith's hospital room, faith tested under fire.

So it happened that on the day I visited Apple Valley, Floyd and Ruth Smith had driven over from Northridge in their camper. Grandfather Smith, slowly putting on weight again, was back to his old chipper self again, taking pleasure and pride in Stacey and her brothers (with such remarks as: "Like the fella says, 'If I'd known how much fun it was to have grandchildren, I'd have had them first' "). And in the hubbub of the Harrison home, Stacey kept the visitor from New York busy, letting me see the poetry she writes, the puppets she creates, the daily writing journals she keeps, all the projects of a young woman who fills her days zestfully and creatively.

There was still another reason for the happy lilt I felt in this family: they had some good news to tell me. On the very day that the telephone call came from *Guideposts* announcing Stacey's contest victory, another call came: the Reverend Donald Harrison was invited to accept a pastorate in Page, Arizona!

And so they were on their way. The Harrison family portrait was complete, a picture of faith triumphant.

Charles Faces His Challenge   ॐ

Helen J. Fricke

With the ringing of the 8:15 bell, two hundred fifty boys and girls began to fill the large study hall of the Upper School at Greenwich Country Day School. This morning's assembly was one of those I had mentally ticketed "very special." Today the finalists in the public-speaking contest among the seventh-grade boys would compete for the coveted Declamation Award. I settled back to enjoy the morning's program.

A hymn. A prayer. The announcement of the four speakers. The contest had begun. First came a rather serious selection, followed by an uproariously humorous one, then an excerpt from a speech by a famous American.

The fourth boy, Charles Neale, slight, dark-haired, was now walking toward the front of the room. By way of introduction, he began:

"I have chosen the story of David and Goliath. It is from the Bible, and its theme is faith. Faith is a simple virtue—but very powerful."

As he began to speak, my thoughts raced over what I knew of this twelve-year-old's background. His father, Hugh Neale, was responsible for the design of a number of atomic power plants and had also developed twenty-three nuclear-reactor designs. Former chief engineer of the atomics division of the American Machine and Foundry Company, he had retired at the age of thirty-seven because of serious illness. For the past several years he had been struggling under the crushing blows of amyotrophic sclerosis (Lou Gehrig's disease).

"And David rose up early in the morning, and left the sheep with a keeper . . . and he came to the trench, as the host was going forth to the fight. . . ."

Occasionally I had lunch with Charles's mother, a remedial teacher, in our school dining room. Although I did not know her well, her gentleness and her ready smile had drawn me to her. It was some time before I had learned—from someone else—of her husband's grave illness.

Her cheerfulness, her honest confrontation with the problems they were facing, the tenderness in her voice when she spoke of the loved one who was becoming increasingly helpless physically, impressed me greatly. Could my own faith sustain me in similar circumstances?

"And Saul said to David, 'Thou art not able to go against this Philistine to fight with him: for thou art but a youth' " (1 Samuel 17:33).

The quiet words were still spoken slowly, clearly, commanding attention. I wondered why his mother had not come to this assembly. They were such a close-knit family, and parents often come on such occasions. It was too bad, I thought, for she would have been so proud of her son.

"Thou comest to me with a sword, and with a spear, and with a shield: but I come to thee in the name of the Lord of hosts. . . . This day will the Lord deliver thee into mine hand . . . and all this assembly shall know that the Lord saveth not with sword and spear: for the battle is the Lord's" (1 Samuel 17:45–47).

Far more than a mere recital of a story from the Bible, Charles was giving expression to a reliance on God found not only in the life of David, but in his own young life and in the lives of his parents.

"So David prevailed over the Philistine with a sling and with a stone" (1 Samuel 17:50).

For the few minutes that he stood there Charles might have been that shepherd boy.

The winner was to be announced later in the dining hall, at the close of the lunch period. I had to leave before then, but an eighth-grader in my class later told me what happened.

"Charles won all right. But we all felt really sad for him when Mr. Webster told us about his father."

"Because his father has been sick such a long time?" I asked. "Didn't you know about that?"

"No. I didn't know. After Mr. Webster made the announcement that Charles had won, he told us that when he had got back to his office after assembly this morning, there was a note on his desk. It was from Charles's mother. Do you know what it said?"

"No," I answered, waiting.

"Well, it said, 'Please excuse Charles after lunch today. His father died last night. He came to school because that is what he felt his father would have wanted.' "

Abducted! 🦢

Delisa Boydston

I thought he was waiting for somebody. He was leaning against a post near my car in the parking lot of a large department store in Pasadena, California, a shabby-looking man in his late forties. "Good afternoon," I said, getting out of my car.

"Hello," he mumbled and looked at the ground. In spite of the pleasant, sunny September day, he seemed gloomy and preoccupied. I forgot all about him as I went into the store. As for myself, I was in a great mood. I'd had a happy start to my day with an early-morning Bible class, and I still had lots to do: see my car insurance agent, buy a gift for a friend's birthday, give a singing lesson at my church.

As I walked around the store, with its bright array of stylish clothing, I looked at the other shoppers—old, young, fat, skinny. I couldn't help but wonder about their relationships with God. Now, I don't usually go around thinking about that, but I'd just completed a course called "Evangelism Explosion," which taught me how to share my faith in Jesus Christ.

I'd worked hard memorizing the complex outline presentation

that was supposed to seem smooth and natural when put to use. Boiled down, it consisted of three main biblical ideas: (1) Convincing a nonbeliever of everyone's need for God (Romans 3:23). (2) Persuading him or her that, in spite of our sin, God is loving and merciful (Jeremiah 31:3). (3) Leading him or her to trust Christ as his or her Savior (Acts 16:31).

I caught my reflection in a mirror on the makeup counter: a young woman of twenty-three—was I really knowledgeable enough to share the gospel effectively? Would I know the right time and place? Would I even remember the main points? Pushing my doubts away, I went about my chores.

As I left the store and went into the parking lot, I passed by the same man I'd seen before, still standing dejectedly by the post. My car was only ten feet away from him. I opened the door, sat down, put my packages on the passenger seat, and was just about to swing my legs into the car when suddenly he was hovering over me, pushing a handbill at me. Just as I started to say no thanks, he roughly grabbed it away again and thrust a knife at me with his other hand. "I'll kill you if you don't move over," he growled.

Suddenly my breath was sucked away painfully. I felt cold all over. Without thinking, I started pushing against him, but the man forcefully shoved me over to the passenger seat of the car. *This can't be happening!* I thought. *It's a nightmare!* I tried to unlock the door, but it jammed. I saw blood running from a cut in my right hand. *O God, help me,* I prayed.

The man got in the car and started it. Then he put his right arm around me and pressed the cold steel of the knife into my neck. "I don't want to hurt you," he said hurriedly. "I just want the car. I'll let you off at the first corner." He ordered me to shift gears, and we peeled out of the parking lot, nearly sideswiping two parked cars.

We zoomed past the corner outside the parking lot and onto the freeway. At that moment I began to panic. I knew he had no intention of letting me go. Never in my life had I experienced such horror and fear. My heart beat in my ears so loudly I was sure he could hear it. I looked at the man fearfully. His right arm was still around my neck and the knife he held seemed sharper by the second. *There is no help,* I thought. *I'm alone with this man, and he's dangerous.*

"Are you married?" he asked.

"Yes," I lied. The question frightened me. I figured if he thought I had a family who'd be expecting my return, he might be more hesitant about harming me.

Then my eyes fell on my Bible in my lap. Here was my lifeline, my salvation! *Lord, I know You're with me always. Please help me to be calm.*

Suddenly, from deep within, I found the courage and inspiration to say, "Would you please take the knife away from my throat? I won't jump out of the car at sixty miles an hour!"

He took his arm away, and I breathed a prayer of thanks—I knew God was truly with me there.

Gaining courage, I asked if I could read from the Bible. He sort of shrugged, "I don't care." I picked up the Bible and noticed that my hand had stopped bleeding; it was only a superficial cut. I fumbled through the pages to the Psalms, amazed that my shaking fingers didn't rip the pages.

" 'The Lord is my shepherd; I shall not want. . . .' " The beautiful words, so peaceful, so deeply comforting, seemed to shiver in the air, so quavery was my voice. " 'Yea, though I walk through the valley of the shadow of death, I will fear no evil. . . .' "

When I finished reading the twenty-third Psalm, the man said to me, "What's all that stuff supposed to mean? I never understood any of it."

Dimly I realized that he was giving me the perfect "opening" for the message of the gospel. Outside the car windows, trees and traffic signs tore past. The details of the evangelism outline I'd so carefully memorized seemed to disappear along with them. *Lord, help me,* I prayed, *if this is what You want me to do.*

I glanced at the Bible in my lap. Just as before, I knew the words of the gospel were my only hope. I sighed deeply and prayed, *Lord, I have a feeling I'm really going to botch that long outline I learned, but help me make some sense to this man. Help me to let him know that You love him.*

"When I say, 'The Lord is my shepherd,' " I began, my voice shaking, "that means that God guides and protects me every step of my life. I believe that God can bring good out of every situation if you love Him—even something like this. There's another quotation in the Bible that says the same thing. I'll read it for you."

He didn't seem to have heard. He glared ahead, gripping the wheel as if he'd break it off. His driving was fast and reckless. It seemed to take me forever to find Romans 8:28 with my trembling fingers. " 'And we know that all things work together for good to them that love God.' "

"Hmph!" the man snorted. Yet when I looked at his face, his expression had changed slightly; it seemed to have softened. "You really believe that?" he asked.

"Yes, absolutely." I began speaking rapidly of my faith in Jesus Christ. "Since I've found Christ, my whole life has changed. No matter what my problems have been, I've felt a new sense of purpose . . . a security in His love and protection . . ." I spoke on and on. Astonishing even myself, I told him that no matter what happened to me—even if he killed me!—I knew I'd go to Heaven.

He just kept staring straight ahead and said nothing.

Then I remembered that, when witnessing, you are supposed to ask the person about himself, to get some idea of what his personal needs are.

"Can you tell me what you're planning to do right now?"

"I- I won't hurt you," he stammered. "I just have to get somewhere."

"Where?"

He didn't answer. I realized then that he really didn't know what he was doing or where he was going. This frightened me just as much as if he had told me he was planning to rape and kill me.

"Look," I said, trying to sound firm, "I have to get back to my church in forty-five minutes to give a singing lesson."

"Well, it takes about an hour to get where we're going."

I took a deep breath. I had to pull myself together to continue to try to persuade him. I gripped the edges of the Bible in my lap, wondering if I was being a complete fool, but knowing the Word of God was my only hope. "Can you tell me what your name is?" I asked. "If you're married?"

"I don't think I should tell you my name. I have a wife and a young son and a daughter about your age. But they're better off without me. I just lost my job. And, see this?"

He extended the inside of his right arm to me. It was riddled with little red marks that looked like insect bites. But with a shock that washed through me like ice water I realized they were needle marks.

"I've spent a lot of time in jail, and I just got off drugs a few days ago. My rehabilitation counselor knows I'm nervous. She told me not to do anything rash—but I had to get this car."

I was amazed at this outpouring. God was truly helping me! The man had told me his fears and anxieties. My only hope now was somehow to meet them with the message of God's love. I prayed that God would speak through me.

"The most important thing you can ever know," I began, "is that God loves you. That's what God is all about—love." I flipped back to Psalm 23. "Where it says, 'my cup runneth over,' that means that we can hardly comprehend His love; it's too much for us to hold. And it says, 'Surely goodness and mercy shall follow me.' He's a merciful God. He loves and forgives everybody, no matter what they do."

I talked about this for a long time. I wasn't sure if he was listening or cared—but I knew I must witness to him. Almost miraculously, Scripture quotations came back to me. "In the New Testament, Jesus tells us that He is the Good Shepherd and that on the cross He laid down His life to save His sheep. That's how much He loves us. That means if we listen to Christ and follow Him, we will live with Him forever in Heaven."

He was very quiet. Then suddenly he took an exit at Pomona and started driving through a run-down old neighborhood. The empty windows of abandoned buildings seemed to leer evilly at me. *This is it,* I thought, *I'm going to die.* Then other bits of the outline started coming back to me: *If the person you are witnessing to seems at all receptive, tell him about a church where he'll be welcome.*

"I go to Lake Avenue Congregational Church, in Pasadena. There are counselors and pastors there who could help you, who'd be willing to talk to you about your problems with drugs and jobs or anything on your mind. I think you ought to take me back there. It's a much better way of dealing with your problems than what you're doing now."

Still, he was quiet. The car rumbled on, bouncing now and then on the uneven streets. I felt the panic rising again, the awful feeling of claustrophobia and helplessness. I prayed, *Lord, keep me calm.*

Then the man said, "I'm thinking about taking you back."

I felt certain I shouldn't speak. I just kept praying to myself, *God, please do something to change his heart.*

All of a sudden the man whipped the car around in a U-turn. "I'm taking you back to your church," he said quietly. He handed me the knife. "Do whatever you want with this. I'd like to hear some more of this stuff about God and Jesus."

I knew he meant it. He sat back in the seat. The very lines of his face had relaxed. In no time we were back on the highway, headed for Pasadena. I was so happy, I sang hymns of praise all the way back to the church.

When we arrived, he parked the car and handed me my keys. "I'd like to talk to the pastor," he said.

Together we went into the church's reception area. Though I was still a little shaky and my hand and neck were bruised and dirty, the receptionist politely seemed to ignore it. "My friend wants to talk to the pastor," I said. "Who's on duty?"

"John," she said.

John Raymond is a down-to-earth, direct man, a good friend of mine. I was totally confident he could handle the situation. We went up the stairs to his office.

As soon as we walked in, the man said, "I'm a drug addict and an ex-convict. I've just abducted this young lady."

John looked from him to me and back again, containing his amazement. "Please sit down," he said. We took seats in front of his desk. I was safe at last.

"Is it true?" John asked me.

"Yes," I said and briefly explained what had just happened. "I've told him about the Lord, that God loves and forgives him. He'd like to know more."

John nodded. Slowly and patiently, he began talking with the man, who told us his name and address. He was open and seemed relaxed. John talked for about ten minutes, presenting the gospel clearly and simply.

"That's just what she told me!" the man said. He seemed surprised and glad, as if relieved to know I hadn't just made it all up.

"Would you like to pray now and ask Jesus into your life?" John asked him.

"Yes, I would. But I don't know how."

"Just repeat after me: Lord, I acknowledge my sins and ask You to forgive me."

Clasping his hands and bowing his head, the man repeated it in a solemn voice.

John continued, "I ask that You enter my heart and live in my life as Lord and Savior now and forever. Amen."

The man repeated that, too. Then he turned to me with tears in his eyes. "I can't tell you how sorry I am for what I did to you." He paused and looked away thoughtfully. "Maybe things do work out for good—like you told me."

He *had* heard!

I decided, after prayer and consultation with John and with the other pastors, not to press charges. John and I believed the man was sincere and that going back to jail would only jeopardize his faith and stability. The pastors have kept in touch with him. He's returned to his family, stayed out of trouble, and got his job back.

How can I sum up what I learned from this extraordinary

experience? That God loves and forgives us all and is with us always. That He works in wonderful ways. Most of all, that He *wants* us to share our faith with others. Just as Jesus said: "Do not worry beforehand about what you will say, but when the time comes say whatever is given you to say; for it is not you who will be speaking, but the Holy Spirit" (Mark 13:11, NEB).

Trusting
Mildred N. Hoyer

Oh, for the faith
    Of a spider
That begins to spin
    The web
Without any thread.

Faith Praises God, No Matter What

Count Your Treasures

Richard H. Jackson

Count your garden by the flowers,
Never by the leaves that fall.
Count your day by golden hours,
Don't remember clouds at all.

Count your nights by stars, not shadows,
Count your life by smiles, not tears,
And, with joy on every birthday,
Count your age by friends—not years.

The Prayer of Praise ट्र

Catherine Marshall

Not too very long ago I reached a low point in life in which everything seemed to go gray. It wasn't all psychological or spiritual grayness, either. Events in the exterior world seemed to be going against me—things like a Hollywood studio purchasing my novel *Christy,* then deciding not to produce it. And the fiction manuscript on which I was working was presenting problems so great that I began to see that after pouring myself into it for three years I was going to have to suspend work on it.

An almost wild succession of small, vexing personal inconveniences came on in waves—the dishwasher broke; the bathroom plumbing went awry; a truck driver backed into our mailbox and demolished it; the lawn developed chinch bugs; the car kept stopping cold on us.

I thought about the Bible passage in which the Apostle Paul says, "In every thing give thanks; for this is the will of God in Christ Jesus concerning you" (1 Thessalonians 5:18). It's one with which I have always had trouble.

I prayed about it in puzzlement. "You mean," I asked the Lord, "that even in the midst of difficult or tragic circumstances, by an act of will I'm to thank You? Wouldn't it just be words, almost hypocritical?"

God's answer was just as direct: "Obedience means turning your back on the problem or the grief and directing your eyes and attention toward Me. Then I will supply the emotion to make the praise real."

So I decided to try to obey. Early one morning I went out on the patio to begin. I had my long list of disappointments, some minor, some deeply tragic. As I stood in the early morning coolness, birds sang in the trees. The sky was still gray-white with the faintest suggestion of blue. I began that first time hesitatingly, woodenly.

"Lord, I think I'll begin with the small irritations first—for example, the truck driver who demolished our mailbox yesterday. Surely I'm not supposed to thank You for *that!* However, I can see as I talk to You that the mailbox is of no consequence. Looking at You puts petty problems into perspective in a hurry."

I persisted on down my list. But as I approached the major

problems and griefs that had been troubling me, I again rebelled.

"Lord, I can see praising You for bringing good out of all these things. But I still don't understand how I can praise You for the bad things themselves."

"I am Lord over all—good and evil," He seemed to answer. "You start praising. I'll supply the understanding."

Step by hesitant step, in the months that followed, I was led on an exciting spiritual adventure.

My first discovery was that I knew almost nothing about praise, neither what it was, nor how to do it. Aside from some joyous hymns and a few we-adore-and-worship-Thee's, most of us church-goers sit so properly in our pews staring straight ahead, how can we know how to praise? Praise is mentioned occasionally as a nice worship exercise; but as a key to answered prayer? That to me was a new concept altogether.

In my adventure, I began to see that God steps in to change unhappy or even disastrous situations in our lives when we thank Him for the situation itself. That makes sense only when we understand that God is "in" every circumstance—good or bad—that He allows to come to us. Growth comes at the point when we take an active step toward God, who stands waiting for us at the center of the problem, and thank Him for it.

The Bible gives us many illustrations of praise being the hinge upon which great events turned. There was the time that Paul and Silas were cruelly beaten at Philippi and jailed in chains. They gave themselves to prayer, which is understandable. But also to joyous praise.

Praise for what? we might ask cynically. That their backs were raw and bleeding? That they were chained fast in prison with all the city authorities against them? Thanking God for *that*? From any human point of view it seems like foolishness.

But Paul says that anything about Christ's cross, or the crosses you and I bear in life, is "foolishness" to the world. Paul learned that God allows us to have disappointments, frustrations, because He wants us to see that our joy is not in such worldly pleasures as success or money or popularity. Our joy is in the fact that we have a relationship with God. Few of us ever understand that fact until circumstances have divested us of any possibility of help except by God Himself.

When Paul and Silas, though bruised and bleeding, turned their minds from self and sang their thanksgiving to the Lord, an earthquake rocked the city of Philippi, shook the prison, burst the gates, and wrenched the chains from the walls. Two other miracles followed quickly. The jailer and his entire household became followers, and when morning dawned, the city authorities withdrew all charges, saying, "Go in peace" (Acts 16).

Here is another incident, one from today. The Redeemer Temple in Denver, Colorado, is an unusual church attended by people of many denominations. On Sunday, May 17, 1970, the sanctuary was crowded. Suddenly a young man stumbled up to the altar. He was obviously drunk. "My name's Clarence," he said. "I'm proud not to be white, proud to be a Black Panther."

Waving a black beret aloft, he began a rambling speech filled with clichés and hate talk. The pastor walked over to the intruder and put one arm around his shoulders. "Clarence, see all those people out there? They love you because they know how much Jesus loves you."

Finally Clarence sat down. But as the pastor began the morning prayer, the drunken man's voice was heard again.

Then a strange thing happened. All over the church, people began softly praising God aloud. "Thank You, Lord" . . . "We praise You for what is happening." When they stopped, Clarence was gone.

But not long afterward, in the same church, Clarence rose and made a public apology for his behavior that day. Then he asked for prayer for himself and for the Black Panther organization. Even in the minor emergency of an interruption of a worship service, praise had wrought its own miracle.

I have begun to see that as we begin praising in each circumstance, ever-fresh insights follow. When we praise, we are letting self go by deliberately turning our backs on the problem or grief where self has been most involved. We stop fighting the evil and less-than-good circumstances. With that, resentment goes. Self-pity goes. Perspective comes. We have turned our back on the problem and are looking steadily at God, at His goodness, His love. The power this gives us in solving our problems and overcoming our obstacles is undeniable.

Soon I also made the discovery that—as nothing else does—thankfulness enables us to live in the present moment. Not often do any of us grasp one shining moment, live fully in its "presentness," and consciously enjoy it. I shall not forget one such moment.

After dinner one evening my mother and I were comfortably

settled in our living room. Around us flowed the music of a fine recording, the London Philharmonic playing Mendelssohn's *Violin Concerto in E Minor*. As we listened, our hands busy making some table mats to be a gift, the singing, soaring melody was a delight.

All at once my heart overflowed with praise. Silently I lifted all of it to God: *This quiet room, the comfort and peace of it. . . . By Your mercy and grace, Lord, Mother is still with us. Isn't it great that we have such rapport that often conversation isn't even necessary? . . . This music, so glorious. Work for my hands to do, work that I enjoy. This moment—what delight!—in the midst of a busy life.*

Later I marveled that such a quiet, unassuming moment had meant so much. *Why?* I wondered.

The word *consciousness* is probably the key. The thankful heart raised in praise and adoration, verbal or silent, becomes the vessel to capture the distilled essence of the presentness of life.

Yes, we gain in many ways when we deliberately plunge a negative situation into the positive Presence of God. The longer I ponder this matter of praise, and experiment with it, the more evidence I see that here is the most powerful prayer of all, a golden bridge to the heart of God.

A Stone Called Ebenezer

Faye Field

I stood in our meadow overspread with black-eyed Susans, pale violets, wild pinks, bluebonnets, goldenrods, and royal-purple sweet williams. Anyone would have called this Saturday morning in April, with its zephyrlike breeze, an extraordinarily enchanting day.

But I did not savor the charm of the beginning season. Instead, I plodded along. I was even unmindful of my favorite spot, the majestic circle of giant, spreading pecan trees surrounding the twin natural springs bubbling with clear crystal water. I failed to admire the Angus cows in the distance looking like dark jewels against the fence bordered by luscious blackberries.

My ears shut out the country sounds I loved so well: the resonant cawing of the crows, the wistful calls of the rain doves, the
cheerful croaking of fat frogs gossiping at the edge of the creek. I
actually stomped deliberately on dew-spangled webs in the fragrant
ankle-deep grass.

I missed the delightfulness of all these things because I was
overcome with dejection. When you're sixteen, disappointment
can be like an avalanche of ruin.

Earlier that morning Papa had asked me to stay at the breakfast
table after the other family members had finished eating. I sat very
still as he drank his second cup of coffee. Papa usually completed
a meal at full speed, ready to hurry-scurry to waiting chores. But
now he actually dawdled, sipping his coffee slowly. He thrummed
the fingers of his left hand nervously against the side of his chair.
It was almost as if he never wanted to empty the cup.

His enormous blue eyes grew even larger, as they did when he
was angry. But he didn't seem angry with *me*. Finally, he spoke,
quietly but firmly, using the nickname he had given me. "Fellow,
the Depression is getting worse, much worse. I have debts to pay.
The crops are not going to be good this year. Papa hates to tell you
this, but I can't send you to college next fall. There's just not
enough money."

I ran outside, sparing him the sight of my tears. I cried as if my
heart would break as I trudged past the pecan trees. When I came
to the path lined with broomweed that led to the Mays's little
cottage, I saw Bumpy John sitting there on the tumbledown steps
whittling.

Wiping away my tears, I moved slowly along to visit with him.
I guess I had seen him like this more than a hundred times, with
his large frame bent over, absorbed in the trimming of a wooden
stick. His long legs were always stretched out over the last step and
onto the ground. Although his hair was graying, it never occurred
to me that he was old.

This beloved man had worked on our farm for many years. He
could carve the most beautiful slingshots. He could plow a perfectly
straight cotton row. But best of all he could tell endless interesting
stories, especially about his boyhood days in "Hell's Half Acre," a
rowdy neighborhood near the stock pens in Fort Worth.

His wife, Willie, had papered their entire house with newspapers held together with flour-and-water paste. You could stand in
one place and read of current events. Or you could go into another

room and read of happenings of bygone days. She also managed to have the most succulent aromas wafting from the wood stove in her small kitchen.

As I sat down beside him, Bumpy John looked up from his whittling. "Good morning, Miss Faye," he said with a wide smile.

I waited awhile before I spoke. I did not want my voice to break. I watched the sun making shady, fascinating patterns on the porch. I heard the homemade front window bobbing back and forth on its worn leather hinges.

At last I responded bluntly, "Not a very good morning for me."

Bumpy John studied my face. "You are pretty when you smile. But, oh my, with that face you are wearing now, I'm glad it's not freezing weather."

Then I poured out my story. "Papa told me this morning he doesn't have the money for me to go to college. I've studied hard and made good grades. I *must* go to college! I want to learn how to write stories. I'm eager to tell about this land, these woods, this farm, and people like you and Willie, Bumpy John. Now all of my dreams are down the drain. I can't bear the thought of missing going to college. What can I ever do?"

This outburst brought Bumpy John's big collie from under the house. The huge dog sidled up to me and began licking my hand.

Bumpy John, perhaps because of his love of the Lord and because he lived so close to nature, possessed a rare sensitivity to life. He said tenderly, "You always say you like to hear me tell stories. I am going to tell you a story now about an Old Testament prophet, Samuel.*

"For a long, long time the Philistines had been fighting against the Israelites. One particular day a large crowd of Israelites got together. They asked Samuel to pray to the Lord to save them from the Philistines. The enemy was right at their door. Samuel prayed. The Israelites were able to mop up the Philistines. Then Samuel put a stone at the border and named it Ebenezer, and he said, 'Hitherto hath the Lord helped us.'

"You know what happened then? The Bible says that after that the Philistines 'came no more.' "

Growing calmer, I asked, "Is that why you named your dog Ebenezer?"

---

*1 Samuel 7:6-13

"Right. But what I want you to remember, Miss Faye, is that this great man, Samuel, never forgot that up to then the Lord had helped them. He knew the Lord would not quit these people now but would keep right on encouraging them.

"Now think like Samuel did. Think of some ways the Lord has helped you up to now. You have a fine family, a nice home, friends; you are healthy. You have good teachers at school; you are the honor graduate of your class. Don't you count these blessings?"

"Yes, the Lord has blessed me in the past," I agreed.

"Well, thank the Lord for what He has done up to now. *Hitherto* is the main word. Your enemies will go away too."

"My enemy right now is lack of money for college," I sighed.

Bumpy John reasoned patiently. "Remember the things right around here. It took some fretting to keep up your dad's farm. Maybe it took the Lord a hundred years to produce this year's crop.

"It may take a while, but the Lord won't leave you now. Let's keep praying like the old prophet did, and you'll see what the Lord can do."

I started home feeling better. That night I read with new under-standing the Bible story of Samuel's faith in this special instance. For weeks after that, I thanked the Lord for his blessings "hith-erto." Each day I felt a calming peace in remembering past bless-ings.

Then one bright day in June some field operators from a lead-ing oil company came and leased our land for a fabulous amount of money. There was plenty for me to attend college that fall, and enough to keep me there until I got my degree. The modern Philis-tines (Depression days) were gone—and came no more to our house.

Now whenever I am discouraged, I conjure up in my mind's eye the scene of a gentle man, an affectionate dog, and an impatient girl sitting together on some rickety steps while a story of faith is warmly told.

And sometimes, when I am mulling over a problem, people may hear me whisper lightly, "Ebenezer."

ॐ

Thank You, God

Mary Ada Peters

At the Masonic Home in Utica, New York, where I am spending the remainder of my life, I am a happy and contented person at the age of eighty-seven.

Several months ago, however, something happened to disrupt this smooth routine. I tripped on the fringe of my bedspread and was thrown across my room. I heard the crunch, and I knew I had broken bones. Indeed, I'd shattered the long femur bone of my leg in three places, all the way from just above the knee to the hip.

After three days of X rays and tests, I went to surgery. They tell me I was on the operating table two hours. Apparently the word got out that I might not live through this experience, and even if I did, it would mean a wheelchair for the rest of my life.

But, after several days of delirium and fever, I came to and gathered my wits about me. I began to talk with God. I said to Him: "If I can be of any help to people worse off than I am, then I want to walk again. Okay?"

Then I began to say the words of a song I used to sing in Sunday school:

"God is love.
That love surrounds me.
In His love, I safely dwell.
'Tis above, beneath, around me.
God is love and all is well."

I sat up on the side of my bed. A nurse came and put me back down.

The next day, I saw a wheelchair over in a corner. I asked the cleaning maid to push it over near my bed. With my strong arms, I swung my body into it, and went for a ride about the hospital ward. I was put back in bed, and soundly scolded.

After that, every chance I got I was in and out; I'd go to the TV room to see my favorite programs. The nurses who saw me thought I must have been given permission.

All this time the words of that song, "God Is Love," ran through my head, and I talked with God and gave thanks.

I progressed from a wheelchair to hopping on a walker, to a cane; and the day came when I returned to my beautiful room here at the Home.

I have thrown away my cane, and I walk without a limp, and I am spending my days with those who need my help. I write letters for those with poor eyesight. I work in the post office mornings.

Thank You, God. I knew we could do it.

Two Simple Remedies

Isla Paschal Richardson

Two simple remedies for life's dark hours
Are gratitude and work, whose soothing powers
A transient sedative in mercy bring,
Until the heart again can learn to sing.

What to Do with a Sleepless Night

Lorna Smith

For years I had trouble going to sleep. I would lie there pressing my eyelids down over wide-awake eyes, trying to relax each muscle, praying. But my mind kept whirling and my eyes kept popping open.

Finally one night I said to myself, *"How stupid! I'm wearing myself out trying to go to sleep. I may as well get up and do something useful."*

Then came the question: How best to use the time? Housework? "No, I do that all day long." Sewing? "Machine too noisy." Suddenly an idea came to me. Why not use these sleepless nights as extra time to do all the things I loved to do and never had time for as a busy wife and mother.

From then on, whenever I found myself tossing and turning, I would lie there till I'd decided just what I'd like most to do. Then I'd get up with joy, thanking God for the extra time He was giving me. Sometimes I would write—letters, a poem, my personal thoughts. Sometimes I'd read, but only what I really wanted to read. Sometimes I'd think of people I knew and of their needs, and pray for them.

As I grew drowsy, I would put away my "playthings" and go back to bed. Some nights I only managed four hours of sleep. But I arose as refreshed as if I'd slept soundly for eight hours. The day after would be delightful. Far from feeling overtired, I tackled my work with zest—not like those wrung-out days when I had fought for sleep half the night.

After a while my gift nights came less and less often. When several busy weeks would pass without one, I would actually catch myself wishing I would not be able to sleep! Isn't that something!

Ordeal in the Mountains

Deborah Dortzbach with Glenn Kittler

It happened without warning. I was walking down the hall of the mission hospital when a masked man with a pistol lunged at me from the shadows.

"Come with me!" he growled, grabbing my arm.

I shrank back, terrified. "Who are you? What do you want?"

"Come!" he repeated. Tightening his grip, he forced me down the hall, through the outpatient clinic, then outside. Why? Who would want a nurse from the American Evangelical Mission Hospital in northern Ethiopia?

Outside, three fierce-looking men held another nurse at rifle point—blond, Anna Strikwerda, from Holland, a friend of mine. Even though I was twenty-four and she fifty-two, we shared much in common and had often prayed together.

"Don't be afraid, Debbie," she called. "They're Eritrean Liberation Front." I remembered that Eritrea, a small country on the Red Sea, had been merged with Ethiopia in 1962. Since then the

E.L.F. army had been waging active warfare to regain independence.

The men closed in, rifles pointed at us. The masked leader barked, "Come on!" Anna and I were shoved into a run. The men ran along, surrounding us; we quickly left the low mission buildings behind.

We headed into the barren, rugged wasteland, the craggy mountains looming before us. Anna and I stumbled often as we hurried over the loose stony ground. We clung to each other, calling upon the Lord to protect us and telling each other not to be afraid. But I was deeply worried about the baby not yet five months within me, and about my husband, Karl, a teacher at the mission. He would be frantic. I could only pray that God would reassure him.

Anna and I continued stumbling over the dusty ground. Heat seared us and rivulets of sweat poured down my back. After about twenty minutes, the leader turned and ordered me to walk ahead of Anna. *Why?* I wondered, hot sweat stinging my eyes as we pushed on. I could hear Anna gasping as she struggled over the rocks. Then I heard her exclaim, "Oh, my shoe————"

A rifle exploded. I wheeled to see Anna fall backward. She lay motionless in the dust. I stifled a scream as my heart cried out for her.

Fear flooded me. Would I be next?

I wanted to scream, to run. Trembling, I turned away . . . and saw the mountains. Then, clearly, as though someone were saying them, words from the Bible came to me: "I will lift up mine eyes unto the hills, from whence cometh my help. My help cometh from the Lord, which made heaven and earth" (Psalm 121).

It was as though a cool hand had been placed on my throbbing temples. A comforting assurance filled me. I distinctly felt the presence of the Lord there with me and knew that if I put my complete trust in Him, He would protect me. I also was given a strong sense that God had given Anna peace and that she was now with Him.

The leader pulled on my arm, motioning me to continue. We began to move even faster as we climbed higher and deeper into the mountains. For two hours we climbed, the men close behind with rifles ready. I tried to fathom the reason for Anna's death; it seemed so ruthless and unreal. Was it because she had difficulty keeping up that the rifleman had in panic pulled the trigger?

I did not want to stumble. I cried to God and kept thanking

Him for keeping up my strength and for His calming presence.

At least we reached a small plateau where a helicopter waited. A leader stood there, a machine gun strapped over his shoulder. He looked at my white uniform, and in English asked, "Are you a doctor?"

So that's what they wanted, I thought.

"No, I'm a nurse."

Much later I was to learn they had wanted a doctor to exchange for a large ransom of medicines and money.

We lifted off and, after roaring over miles of desert, later descended toward what seemed to be a temporary nomad settlement. I was taken to a hut that was to be my home.

Fear welled in me again as I wondered what they would do with me, but again I felt God's comforting presence.

For a few days I was allowed to move around the settlement. The women welcomed me into their primitive huts and let me examine their children. The little ones suffered from malnutrition; the older ones from tuberculosis. I deeply regretted not being able to help them.

Days passed and still I had no idea of what would happen to me. Would I ever see my husband again?

My only refuge was prayer and meditation upon God's word. At times I was so aware of the vivid presence of God that I had to sing out. One day I began to sing "He's Got the Whole World in His Hand." As I did, villagers gathered around me, their eyes sparkling. Soon they were clapping their hands in rhythm with me and trying to pick up the tune.

Later three E.L.F. men, who knew some English, wanted to talk politics. "I can understand that your country has many problems," I said, "but if you want real freedom, you must seek it in Jesus. He was the greatest revolutionary. He came into the world to free people from the slavery of sin."

They didn't say anything. But when I walked away, they began speaking Tigré. I heard them say the name of Jesus several times. Was a seed planted?

On the tenth day, the leader said they'd be moving on.

"Can I go back to the mission?" I asked.

"Not yet," he said, and then I learned that I was to move yet deeper into the mountains. "When it is time for you to leave there, I will send a messenger."

There was nothing I could do. Early the next morning we began traveling by mule the several miles through the mountains to a small lean-to.

Days passed, each longer than the one before it. The guards kept to themselves. The solitude began to eat into me. It had now been two weeks since I had been taken away from my husband and friends.

"How long, O Lord, how long?" I cried. I thought of Elijah's two years alone by the Brook Cherith and how his food was brought to him each day by a raven.

Could I survive two years here? Just then I heard a croaking in the sky and looked up. Incredibly, circling above me was a raven. "Oh, thank You, God," I cried, "for Your sign of nearness."

I began to suffer terribly from idleness. I prayed, and a thought came to me. I knew that people in this area made and repaired their own clothes. I went to my guards and indicated by gestures what I wanted. One guard lent me his needle. Earlier I had been given two pieces of cloth—a large white piece and a striped, colored piece. I reduced the colored cloth to threads and entwined them to make a multicolored yarn. With the needle I was then able to embroider Bible verses that kept going through my mind.

It kept me focused on God and gave me another way to pray.

Then one day, three weeks after I had been taken captive, a messenger arrived with a box. It was from my mission and contained canned food and clothes. Now I realized that Karl knew I was alive.

I continued my embroidery work, thankful I had something to do. I thought a lot about home and Karl.

And then, on the twenty-second day, a messenger arrived with a letter from the E.L.F. leader. I was free, though no ransom had been paid.

We left early the next morning and spent the first day working our way back through the mountains by muleback. It was rough going and I wondered about the baby. But I also kept thanking the Lord every step of the way, realizing that I was in His care. Then, at another settlement, the mule was exchanged for a camel.

The camel lurched and swayed like a ship in a storm. It was sickening, especially in my condition. But I knew that every step brought me closer to home. Finally, on the twenty-sixth day, we reached a camp. A jeep had been brought to take me the rest of the way to a town. There I was able to telephone Karl.

Soon Karl and I were in each other's arms. "Darling," he cried, "are you and the baby all right?"

Smiling through my tears, I handed him the white cloth I had embroidered. On it he read my answer—"I will lift up mine eyes unto the hills, from whence cometh my help. My help cometh from the Lord, which made heaven and earth."

Prayer

George Herbert (1593–1633)

Thou hast given so much to me,
Give one thing more—a grateful heart.

Faith Changes You and Your World

The Guest

Author Unknown

Faith came singing into my room
And other guests took flight.
Grief and anxiety, fear and gloom
Sped out into the night.
I wondered that such peace could be,
But faith said gently, "Don't you see
That they can never live with me?"

Put Some Lion in Your Life

The Editors

Call it spirit, confidence, or just plain boldness, but a lot of us feel shortchanged on this vital attribute when:

The minister offers us an important church job and we back out gasping that we don't measure up.

We come up with a brilliant new idea for our company, but our enthusiasm goes *phftt* when we face selling it to management.

We see a wrong that should be righted, but shrink into our corner afraid to stick our neck out.

So? Often, someone with less ability or scruples steps in and takes over. And we let down God, our fellows, and ourselves. All because we lack boldness.

Do we really? Do we lack boldness when God gave us the power to fight to survive when we were born, to scream for oxygen, to cry for food? Of course not. But along the way it's often smothered.

A doctor once confessed he'd been plagued with timidity since his boyhood. His parents were devoted and loving but timorous. They lived in constant fear for their son and infected him with their fears. These plagued him all through his school days, medical school, and even through his internship. Finally he decided that he could never heal people's bodies unless he became healed in his own mind. So he sought a medicine that would cure him of his fears.

He found it in the Bible. "I came across a great healing combination of words," he said. "I took them; they permeated my mind and healed me of my fears."

His tonic for timidity: "Be strong and of good courage; be not afraid, neither be thou dismayed: for the Lord thy God is with thee whithersoever thou goest" (Joshua 1:9).

Since human beings first cowered before the dark unknown, God has understood our timidity. Therefore, as the ancient writer tells us, He Himself goes with us. He *wants* us to be bold for Him, to overcome evil, to live our lives to full fruition, to fulfill His plan in the world.

We offer you here some building blocks to boldness. Use them to construct a dynamic new life. Approach each challenge by first asking yourself:

Is it right with God? If so, all the power of heaven and earth is *with* you. The Apostle Paul, while a prisoner aboard a ship sailing for Rome, was caught in a storm. Soon Paul, a landlubber, was boldly giving the captain advice, for Paul knew God's will. And his words rang with such conviction that captain and crew obeyed him unquestioningly, and all hands were saved. We can attain this same conviction by first seeking God's will in all that we wish to accomplish. So ask Him in prayer if your goal is right. If you sense affirmation, then take the next step:

Be bold, and mighty forces will come to your aid. This great truth, so well expressed by author Basil King, has powered many people to success. The idea is to commit yourself by biting off more than you *think* you can chew, rather than letting fear of failure stop you from trying at all. A small boy found his path blocked by an "unclimbable" wall, but he soon scaled it, astounding his friends. When asked how he did it, he said, "I threw my cap over the wall, and then I *had* to get it."

Those "mighty forces" that come to one's aid? They are the deep-down powers we all possess—energy, skill, sound judgment, creativity, even physical strength and endurance in far greater measure than we realize. Boldness creates a state of emergency to which these powers respond. Promise you'll finish the job "next Wednesday," and your pride, competitive instinct, and sense of obligation will see that you do.

Once committed, though, make sure you:

Don't look over your shoulder. Or, as baseball's great Satchel Paige said, "You may see something gaining on you." That "something" could be the fears you overcame at the start. Hesitation and second thoughts can bog you down. So keep up your momentum.

Instead of stopping for doubts:

Make the leap of faith. Often we back away from opportunities because we're afraid we'll make a mistake or get hurt. A businessman tells how early in his career he had an opportunity that, if taken, meant giving up what security he had already achieved. He went out into the city park to think about it.

He had decided not to risk it when he noticed a squirrel in a tree overhead. It, too, faced a moment of decision as it hesitated at the end of a branch. Then, seemingly mustering up courage, it gave a great leap, sailing through space to another tree. The man realized that it was through its leap of faith that the squirrel swiftly advanced from one tree to another.

In Jesus' parable of the talents, the servant who buried his employer's money was criticized for failing to put it to use. The servant's alibi sums up too many people's attitude toward life: "I was afraid to risk it. . . ."

Don't duck the spotlight. Many people shrink from responsibility because they don't want to be noticed. This false timidity often produces its own minor tragedies. An elderly woman is struggling with many packages on a wind-swept street. Of the men hurrying by, most may want to help, but hesitate. For it would mean drawing attention to oneself, and it's more comfortable to remain in the anonymity of the crowd. Yet they'll feel a flash of admiration for the one person who does stop to help.

The next time you hear a call for volunteers or see someone who needs assistance or spot a wrong that needs righting, remember Edmund Burke's words: "The only thing necessary for the triumph of evil is for good men to do nothing."

True boldness should not be confused with pride, effrontery, or aggressiveness. Rather, one should strive for the boldness expressed by a wisp of a woman who in comforting dying men on the battlefield expanded the concept of nursing; by a humble raw-boned boy of the prairie who led his country through its deepest crisis; and by a doctor whose reverence for life brought compassion to those least likely to know it. This is the boldness for which we were born, the boldness that shouts: "Thy will be done, on earth as it is in Heaven!"

From Sour Cream to Sweet Success

R. Gene Scalf

B-r-r-a-a-n-g! I grabbed the alarm clock and was ready to hurl it to the floor when I remembered we couldn't afford a new one. It was 3:00 A.M. I crawled out of bed, trying not to awaken my wife and infant daughter. As my feet touched the cold floor, I grunted to myself, "This is going to be another lousy day!"

Why not? Almost every preceding day had been lousy. Now, at age thirty, I was convinced I was a born failure. After high school in Kentucky, I had piddled at jobs for three years until the Korean

War came along. On completing service, I located in southern California where I finished college and then entered the plastics manufacturing field. I failed at it.

Now I had a home-delivery milk route. I grumbled as I walked out into the inky night to my truck. The truck was lousy too. At each stop, the engine would die.

My first delivery that morning ran true to form. Waiting in an empty bottle was a note like so many others I'd got lately: "Please do not leave any more milk."

At the next house I wondered if I should leave any milk at all. They owed me a good-sized bill. But the battered tricycle by the steps made me hesitate. "What the heck," I said to myself, "I might as well go under in style."

But losing another customer decided me. I'd dump the route. Later that day as I sat in a restaurant staring into a cup of black coffee, a friend tapped me on the shoulder. "Why so glum, Gene?"

"You'd be glum too!" I muttered. And then through three cups of coffee I unloaded my frustrations. "I just can't take it anymore, Ralph," I concluded.

He looked at me quizzically, then said, "I'd like to give you a book to read." I stopped at his house that afternoon to pick it up. It was on positive thinking. I didn't need that kind of book. I needed something to tell me how to run a better milk route.

But I started reading it that night. And something funny happened; the more I read, the more sense it made. One point the author made especially hit me: *Expect the best and get it.* He used a Bible verse: "If thou canst believe, all things are possible to him that believeth" (Mark 9:23). I knew the verse, but wasn't it something for the apostles in those long-ago Bible days? And yet I began to realize that I'd been proving it works, by following it in reverse. Every day I'd expect the worst, and usually got it.

I thought back to why I entered the plastics field, and the milk route: I'd heard of men who were making a success in both. If there was nothing wrong with the jobs, there must be something wrong with me.

So my failures had resulted not from circumstances, but from my negative attitude toward life. And this wasn't just a friend telling me this—every point he made originated in the Bible, which I began to read. "Ask and it shall be given you; seek and ye shall find" (Matthew 7:7)." "For God hath not given us the spirit of fear; but of power, and of love, and of a sound mind" (2 Timothy 1:7).

Yet, could just *thinking* right bring back lost customers, pay up accounts? Crazy as it then seemed, I decided to take a different attitude toward my job. I'd start out each morning saying, "I like my job! This is going to be the greatest day of my life!"

Before long, those words repeated over and over started to become *reality*. I began to see that if I didn't believe in myself, neither could I expect anyone else to. I took another look at my dairy products; they were of excellent quality and people needed them.

Sure, the old truck still sputtered, and "no-thank-you" notes greeted me. But I'd found a strange new power within myself. I started stopping at houses I passed up before, telling housewives how fresh my products were and what a variety I had to offer. With those behind in their accounts, I was frank, but sympathetic. I told them I, too, was short of money, but if they'd just pay me in small installments, we'd work it out.

All I can say is that I began to get more customers and my collections improved. My job actually started becoming *fun*, especially in meeting people along the way.

Before, I'd just grunt as I met customers in making deliveries. But I was *seeing* more now, like the flowers in the yards. I'd tell people how much I enjoyed them, and they'd look as if they'd just won first prize at a flower show.

In time I accepted a better opportunity with a manufacturing company. I found that my improved attitude that had helped my milk route worked just as well in selling laminated plastics.

In my first year I had quadrupled the sales volume in my territory. Within a year and a half I was regional sales manager.

Sure, I still had low periods—when you get so blue you think the whole world is against you. But I learned to recognize this as a normal cycle we *all* go through. Though Babe Ruth hit 714 homers, he also had 1350 strikeouts, and who remembers those? After all, I figure success is not the goal but a pathway on which to travel. And the best way to keep steam up, I've found, is to share with others the enthusiasm God gives us.

The other day I pulled in for gas where I used to have my milk truck serviced. "Fill it up, George," I said. "It's a great day, isn't it?" He groaned, "You wouldn't say that if *you* just had two men quit!"

"Well," I said, "if you didn't have problems, the company wouldn't need you. Besides, now you can hire two men better than the two you just lost!"

He grinned. "By golly, I never looked at it that way."

As I drove off, I breathed, "Thanks, Lord—thanks for helping me look at everything this way."

How to Succeed without Trying To Do It All Yourself

Allan Hartley

Early in life I thought I'd learned the secret of success—hard work! Certainly this was the code of my father, Fred Hartley, who served for more than twenty years in the United States Congress. Dad believed that a nation's welfare, like a family's, depended on the energy and efforts of its members.

His philosophy was even reflected in the religion he passed on to me. I remember the night after my grandfather died—Dad's father, whom he loved deeply. The casket was still in our living room, people coming and going, when Dad laid his hand on my shoulder.

"There is nothing after the grave, Allan," he said. "Heaven and hell are right here on earth and it's up to us to make it one or the other."

If I noticed the wistfulness in his voice, I didn't think about it at the time. I was wrapped up in plans for my own career in drawing comics. I landed a job illustrating comic books. I worked hard, I married a beautiful girl, we had two children; it was going to be the great American success story.

But it didn't work that way. Contrary to all my theories, the harder I worked, the worse—in terms of earnings anyway—I seemed to do. The whole comics industry in the late 1940s was in a decline. Parent-teacher groups accused comic books of promoting violence, and although the particular publisher I worked for was not especially guilty, all comic book sales were hurt. Then came TV, and by the 1960s sales had plunged still further.

So I began developing independent projects to augment our income, hurling myself into one enterprise after another, using the formula that energy equals success. I tried designing and selling greeting cards. I illustrated books. I published books of my own. I fell into bed each night exhausted and waking each morning with a churning, anxious stomach.

My wife, Hermine, was dismayed by all this hyperactivity, which cut more and more into our family time. She was perfectly content, she assured me, with what the comic book work brought in. What was I trying to prove by killing myself? No matter how hard a person worked, she pointed out, some things were beyond his control.

She reminded me of the Kennedy cards. In 1963 I had designed and manufactured a deck of playing cards that featured members of the Kennedy family in place of the king, queen, and jack faces. It was an amusing novelty that looked like it was catching on—when suddenly the President's assassination made it unthinkable.

But I couldn't accept the thought that forces outside myself could have the last word. If I just stayed up a little later, worked a little harder . . . With each disappointment I redoubled my activity, neglecting my family still more, neglecting sleep, neglecting God.

During all this time, in spite of the fact that I went to church every Sunday—I was even chairman of our local board of deacons—God played no part in my real, Monday-through-Saturday world. Churchgoing, if I was honest with myself, was for me simply part of the whole successful man syndrome, a place to see and be seen by other men-on-the-rise. As for expecting God to get involved in the grubby details of my business life—I had no inkling that He would or should do such a thing. A man's success was up to him, wasn't it?

It was when my skill and hard work were failing most miserably that some friends invited us to a service at their church. I don't even remember what the sermon was about. I only know that six words suddenly came through. "With God," the minister said, "all things are possible" (Mark 10:27).

Was that true?

Friday morning I was sitting in that minister's study, pouring out my sense of failure and panic. "Wednesday night you said something about all things being possible with God. Does that mean even things like this?"

"All things," he repeated gently. "But you can't ask the Lord to take over just your business or just your health or just your marriage. You must put Him in charge of your entire life."

And so, because I was tired and beaten and frightened, I did that. Driving back to my house that morning, I told Jesus that I, who was never going to ask any favors, was asking the ultimate favor of all. I'd run things myself for forty years and made a mess; now I asked Him to run them for me.

It was the week after I'd made that decision that I learned about a new job from my boss at the comic book publishing house. I was offered a monthly feature for a men's magazine, a comic strip for adults featuring a scantily dressed blonde. It was a well-paying job and just a few days before I would have jumped at it. Now, though, I'd asked God to take over.

Of course I gave myself all the usual arguments. If I didn't do it, someone else would; I could probably make it less objectionable than the next guy. But in the end I knew I was hedging and I turned it down. In the comics field that was suicide. There were always more artists than there were jobs and an artist who got choosy was finished. My boss fired me.

I should have been frantic. I should have started pushing doorbells, writing letters, and phoning everyone I'd ever met to find another job. Instead I was conscious only of an incredible inner peace.

I had been in the comic book field for eighteen years by then and never once in all that time had anyone phoned me with a job offer. Two weeks after I lost my job Archie Enterprises called. How would I like to work for them?

To anyone inside the field, this call-from-the-blue was unaccountable. Archie, created in 1938, was the most successful comic character in the world, selling more than sixty million magazines a year. They hired only four original-drawing artists and probably had four hundred applicants for the jobs. Why telephone someone who'd never applied to them at all?

But the new job was only the beginning. Better still, God gave me a new way to relate to people in terms of His love for them.

Life under His management was so great I found myself wanting to talk about it—and again observed how He arranges all things. No one's ever heard of Allan Hartley, but "the man who draws Archie" was soon getting invitations to youth groups, women's clubs, men's luncheons, until I was speaking about my beliefs several times a week.

Of course this meant time away from my drawing board; but I began to notice a strange thing. My production for eighteen years had been about average for the comics industry—three pages a day. Now, as opportunities to speak meant less time to draw, I found myself producing six pages every day I worked. When speaking dates were extra heavy, I could sometimes finish ten pages a day— and by now I was the only one on the staff writing Archie's adventures as well as illustrating them.

Unlike everything I'd believed all my life, everything my father believed, this increased output was not the result of increased effort. In fact, the old sense of straining had gone altogether. It was as if the true key to accomplishment was not how hard I drove myself, but Who was in control.

The most recent example is an idea I could never even have

thought of myself: Christian stories—stories from the Bible, stories of real people living today—told in comic book form for all the kids who read nothing else. I've even started a series of Christian adventures starring all the Archie gang, with the blessing of my boss at Archie Enterprises, John Goldwater.

I would never have suggested such an idea on my own. But God seemed to be telling me to ask. So I did, and Mr. Goldwater was not only willing but delighted. He told me he'd started Archie back in 1937 hoping to bring a wholesome influence to American homes.

Since I stopped relying on my own cleverness, it's amazing how things have worked out. The whole family's noticed it. In fact, twenty-six relatives have had a deep spiritual change take place in their lives—among them, my fighting warrior of a father. Without God, Dad's last years would have been grim indeed; for this energetic self-reliant man, who'd never depended on anyone else for a thing, suffered a series of strokes, each one leaving him more helpless.

He spent his last four months in Atlantic City General Hospital totally paralyzed, unable even to swallow, dependent on tubes and jars. But his eyes—those eyes that had looked so hopelessly on his father's coffin—shone with certainty that death was not the end.

I remember the last words he ever spoke to me. They came slowly, woodenly; his tongue would not move the way he wanted it to. His breath was shallow; I had to bend close to hear him whisper, "I am very, very happy."

The Man Who Waged Peace

Jacques Clementin

At the time the friendship with Afif seemed like such a small personal thing. When I first received my orders to Algeria, my wife and I had decided we didn't want to be one of those French army families who never got to know Arabs. We even said a prayer about it, asking God to show us how to make friends.

Of course, once settled in Sidi bel Abbès, it didn't look quite so simple. I was there, as a captain in the French army air force, to put down a revolt by Algerian nationalists who wanted independence from France. Those nationalists, who called themselves the FLN, were particularly harsh on fellow Arabs who showed pro-French sympathies—so that even if someone felt personally drawn toward Yvonne and me, he would scarcely dare show it.

Then one day a tradesman named Afif came to our house to install a bottle of cooking gas. Once again Yvonne struggled to get a conversation going. She referred to our own faith in God and to our conviction that He had some better solution to the problems between Algeria and France than to shoot each other. At first Afif remained impassive. Then suddenly, at the doorway, he blurted out that he too was a believer in God.

It was a tiny breakthrough. There followed other visits in his shop or at our home. One day Yvonne and I, with our baby son, Marc, drove out to a suburb of Sidi bel Abbès where Afif lived with his six children in a one-room home. There was no running water and his white-veiled wife prepared our mutton couscous on an open air hearth.

And that, seemingly, was the end of it. Shortly afterwards, the army posted me to the large Algerian port city of Oran, some seventy-five miles from Sidi bel Abbès, and we drifted out of touch.

Meanwhile the fighting in Algeria had taken a new and ugly turn. Back home in France, public sentiment was veering toward granting independence to Algeria. But the large French-settler population in Algeria, whose families had lived there three and four generations, could not accept this. Seeing the mother country waver, those French-Algerians took matters into their own hands. They formed an illegal secret army, the OAS, sworn to continue the fight against the Arab nationalists.

So now the official French army, of which I was a part, confronted not only the Arab revolutionaries, the FLN, but this new force. One day the OAS dynamited a Moslem shop. The FLN retaliated by destroying a French warehouse, and the bloodbath was on. Before long the city was sandbagged off into Arab sectors and people were shot—men, women, even children—who strayed too close to the barriers.

Marc was now two, old enough to be terrified by the dozens of dead and dying who lay every morning on the streets. Yvonne and Marc flew home to France, and I moved out to bachelor quarters at La Senia air base outside the city.

It was there that the letter reached me. It was from a man

Yvonne and I had met at a Moral Re-Armament conference a few years earlier, and in it he asked the question, "What are you personally doing to stop the bloodshed?"

I wrote back a patient letter describing the deep-seated racial and religious conflicts that had led to the present tragedy. His answer did not even allude to all my information. Had I asked God, he repeated, what I individually was to do?

Well—no, I hadn't. I hadn't because it had simply never occurred to me that I—or any other single person—could have an effect on so huge a problem. When I did ask the question in my prayer time the following morning, an answer popped instantly into my mind. I was to bring about a meeting between the FLN and the OAS.

Of course I rejected it instantly. I was just a captain, not at all a man of importance. I had no power, no influence, no connections. Or—did I? A tenuous connection, to be sure, but I knew another man who believed in God—Afif.

So I took a first step. I flew my helicopter to Sidi bel Abbès and went to Afif's house. All I found there was a heap of rubble. The house had been leveled to the ground by my compatriots in the OAS. What a gullible fool I'd been to think that by some individual effort I could make a dent in ancient hatreds.

But back in my barracks room at La Senia, there was the letter, still on my table. "What are you personally doing . . . ?" So once again I asked God, and again I seemed to get an answer, no more sensible than the first. I was to write Afif a letter. But, even supposing he was still alive, there was no house at his address anymore. Still, the idea would not go away.

A few days later I held Afif's answer in my hands. And a few days after that I was sitting with Afif in his refugee home in Tlemcen describing the incredible thought that had come to me of a face-to-face meeting between the FLN and the OAS. When I had finished, Afif spread his great work-scarred hands apart. "It is good. I will try to get in touch with the FLN."

Now I turned my prayers to the next question. How was I to contact the OAS? This time the Lord led me to our own base chaplain who knew people who knew people, and one day I found myself in a dingy apartment in one of the poorer French suburbs of Oran, confronting a French Algerian whose set jaw and perfunctory handshake told me he viewed me with icy suspicion. Why was I, a captain in the official French forces, seeking a rendezvous with the illegal OAS? Was it a trick to discover their leadership?

Then I saw the first thing that encouraged me. In a corner of the shabby room was a small statue of the Virgin Mary. I told the man that I too was a Christian, told him of my growing conviction that God could use individuals, like him and me, who believed in Him, to bring about His will.

At these words, to my astonishment, the stony-faced man began to cry. "I believed the French cause was God's cause," he said brokenly. "But no, this killing cannot be His way. I will help you to talk to our leaders."

And then, suddenly, the bitter affairs of Algeria were no longer my concern. New orders had come through for me. I was to report at once to a special training school in England. At last I would be reunited with my family. I was booked aboard the flight that left Oran Friday night at 7:40.

This was Tuesday. Four days in which to find others who would take over the business of nighttime car trips and whispered phone conversations. But to my great confusion, in my prayer time next morning I got a clear feeling. *No. It is not others. It is you who are to carry on this task.*

How could that be! I had my orders, something a military man could not simply ignore. Supposing though that those other orders came from God? I went to my colonel and requested release from the new assignment. He stared at me as if I were mad. The English appointment was a plum, a great step forward in my career. "You must leave as ordered," he said. "If you are not on that plane, you will be placed under arrest."

I returned to my barracks conscious only of relief. I had done my best; the matter had been taken out of my hands. Too bad too, because the very next day I learned that the bishop of Oran himself was going to try to get my proposal to the OAS leadership.

Friday morning came. There was just time to fly to Tlemcen with the young pilot who had agreed to take my place in the negotiations—a courtesy visit so he and Afif would know each other.

But at Tlemcen we were met with great excitement. Afif and his friends had just now succeeded in setting up a meeting between me and the commandant of all FLN troops in the Oran region. The meeting was set for tomorrow.

So I had to tell them. "Tomorrow," I said, "I shall be in England." I glanced away rather than meet the look of betrayal in their eyes. In vain they pointed out that a substitute would be an insult.

"I am truly sorry," I said, "but I have done everything possible."

To sharpen my sense of failure, back at La Senia another piece of news was waiting for me—a message from the bishop of Oran. The OAS had agreed to a meeting.

It was now an hour and a quarter before my flight. And so in this impasse, as so often in the past weeks, I turned to God. And immediately got the idea—go to General Katz. He's the one man who could change my orders. At 6:30 on Friday evening? Surely the general would have left by now.

Ten minutes later I was standing in front of the general. For some reason, he said, he had put off leaving that evening. And so, blushing to the roots of my hair at the presumptuous sound of it, I confessed that I had been trying to set up top-level talks between the OAS and FLN. The general stared at his desk.

"It might work," he said at last. "It just might work." He looked up. "Keep that appointment with the FLN tomorrow."

The next few days were a blur of faces and journeys. The ride with Afif over deep-rutted roads to the Arab hideout in the mountains. The frightened faces of the FLN leaders the next day as they laid down their weapons and climbed into my helicopter for the flight to Oran. My final drive through the city dark with the smoke of blazing oil tanks to arrange details with the OAS.

And then the unforgettable moment when we all walked through the great double doors of the civic conference room— Frenchmen and Arabs, Christians and Moslems, the bishop, the mayor, the leaders of the FLN and the OAS. The first words of Bakhti, the nationalist leader, set the tone.

"For seven years," he said, "I have been waiting for this moment."

In the peace negotiations that followed there in that top-floor room, I took no part. My role was over, just one of many parts making up a whole no one could see. I let my eyes roam out the windows; the sky was still dark with black, oily smoke, but for the first time in many months there was no sound of shooting. *Yes,* I thought, *One sees the whole. He sees it all, and for this He set the parts in place.*

Editor's note: *Several weeks later, a truce was made and French President Charles de Gaulle declared Algeria independent four months later, on July 3, 1962.*

The Accident That Saved Our Plant ᙥ

Wayne T. Alderson

Bitterness still seemed everywhere. A crippling strike that began in October 1972, and lasted eighty-four days, was finally over; but its ugly scars covered the foundry like casting strips.

In my office I watched the men go by. *Pittron,* I thought, *is like its product—a melting pot.* There are whites, blacks, conservatives, liberals, and militants working here. Put them in a place that's tough, grim, smelly, hot, and extremely dangerous and you've got a potential nightmare.

With gas lines and hot molten steel all about, you've got to be very careful in almost any job you do in the foundry. Even aside from risks, a foundry can be a cruel place. I've seen it get the best of a good man—break him and turn him into an angry animal. The strike did that and even after it ended, there was still great rancor. The place was alive with grumbling, quarreling, disgusted men who hated getting up in the morning. I knew another walkout would close down the plant for good.

As vice-president of Pittron, I had the job of handling employee relations at the plant. It proved to be the toughest part of my work. Men would come to see me and complain about everything. They didn't like their jobs. They hated working with men of another color. The strike had torn apart their families. They wanted more money. They wanted better safety measures in the foundry. They wanted help with their drinking problems.

I would sit at my desk and feel helpless. What could I do? How could I help? I remember when one worker came in and told me his wife wanted a divorce. I listened as he poured his heart out, but I couldn't seem to help.

I knew I had to do something—be more concerned—but I didn't know how. I knew in my own life that whenever I got uptight about something, angry, or ticked off, I could calm myself by reading the Bible and praying. *Of course,* I thought, *that doesn't apply to these men.* I couldn't tell them to do what I did. Then one night while I was searching the Scriptures I came across a verse that really moved me: "If anyone publicly acknowledges me as his friend, I will openly acknowledge him as my friend before my Father in heaven" (Matthew 10:32, TLB).

Jesus's words seemed written just for me. I knew sharing His love, or witnessing, was part of being a Christian, but I wasn't sure it was right for this situation. I certainly didn't want to use Christianity in the foundry. It would be a cop-out and besides I'd be putting my job on the line. I'd always been told religion had no place in the business world.

Yet that Bible verse kept sneaking back to me. I soon saw it wasn't a matter of getting the men to listen—it was a matter of my strengthening my own faith and then taking a stand based on my own convictions.

Slowly, ever so slowly, I began telling the complaining men that perhaps they should bring their problems before God instead of bickering about them. When I told one man how, because I believed in the Lord, He had provided for me, I got a look of annoyance. Some asked questions, others ignored me. But I began to feel much better about myself.

One morning a worker asked me what I thought about the chances of starting a Bible study group in the foundry. I stared at the man. Could this be an answer? I decided to ask around. When a few others were in favor, we went ahead.

We held the study during the lunch shift—a tough time to get anybody to do anything except eat and rest. Our chapel was a damp, converted storage room. Attendance was sparse—to many men, work was bad enough without bringing God into the picture.

Even though the Bible study group grew, I still sensed an unsettled, skeptical feeling in the foundry. I continued to pray for God's guidance.

"Lord," I said, "we feel Your presence here so much more now—but help us to find *real* love and understanding in this place."

His answer to my prayers came in a most unexpected way.

It was a Friday afternoon last November [1973]. About 4:00 P.M., a fifty-five-ton ladle of molten metal was being readied to pour into a casting mold. This is a hazardous operation and much caution goes into it. One little slip and the foundry can turn into an inferno.

Three men on an overhead crane were moving the ladle into place over a mold. As the handle was pulled to release the stopper rod in the huge ladle to start the metal flowing, the rod suddenly snapped and plunged like a rocket through the slag crust on top of the metal.

Liquid fire raced everywhere. The fire engulfed the crane, but the three men inside somehow were able to leap to safety down a catwalk. Meanwhile, the swaying ladle slammed against the wall of the foundry, barely missing overhead oxygen and natural-gas lines. In a few short minutes a two hundred-foot-wide area was ablaze. For fifteen harrowing minutes part of the foundry was like the crater of an erupting volcano.

Then, just like that, it was all over. The fires were brought under control without anyone's being injured. Apparently one of the fleeing cranemen had jarred a lever that kept the ladle from hitting the gas line. Had it hit the line, the foundry would have been reduced to rubble in seconds.

When I got to the scene, John Bradley, an electrician who'd seen it, told me, "It's got to be a miracle!" *Miracle*—that was a word I would hear a lot in the next few days. These were men who knew the perils of foundry work. They knew to escape something like an accident with a careening ladle of steel was unheard of—and miracle was the only explanation.

The following Tuesday three hundred workers stopped operations for a few minutes to hold a thanksgiving service in the chapel. I was there and heard man after man stand up and praise God for sparing so many lives.

Husky Sam Piccolo, the labor union president, said softly, "I've got a purpose here now 'cause I know it was the hand of God on us last Friday. When He's with us, we can do anything."

Ed McKivitz, a melter foreman who was directly underneath the ladle that day, said, "I really got to thank Him for protecting us."

With misty eyes the men joined hands. I read from Isaiah: "When you shall pass through the fire, you shall not be burned, the flame shall not hurt you, for I am the Lord your God" (43:2).

It was a glorious and moving moment and from it seemed to come a new sensitivity among the workers. Men began to take pride in their jobs. Worker complaints lessened. Union relations no longer seemed strained. The men smiled more. The Bible study, once a controversial issue, has now taken on greater meaning.

The other day I was walking through the plant when I noticed a cut-out fish design someone had nailed to a supporting column. On the next column was another fish and so on, leading a path to the chapel. The fish is the same symbol early Christians drew on posts of catacombs to identify themselves as those who belonged to the Lord.

I can now understand the great value in passing on the spirit of the Lord. As for me, I never felt as close to Him, never felt a stronger faith in Him, until I began to tell others about what He can do.

I also know now that God's great love and work can go anywhere—even to the dark and dangerous depths of a steel foundry.

Now when I look up and see smoke coming from a foundry chimney, I think not just of men straining and sweating—but also of men whose hearts have been touched and whose vigor for living has been restored.

"Heal Me, O Lord"

Marilyn Ludolf

I woke up with the same tormenting headache I'd gone to bed with, and struggled to the bathroom. I grasped the sink with both hands and reluctantly raised my pounding head to stare in the mirror. The face reflected in the glass was a fiery red mask of tiny bumps and large acnelike sores. Hundreds of them. The horrible rash covered my face like the Egyptian plague of boils in the Bible. The unending headache and rash comprised the mysterious condition I'd lived with for twelve long, unbearable years. A plague that had appeared out of nowhere when I was thirty-two years old. It had grown steadily in intensity, until here I was a middle-aged woman with two teenaged sons and a husband who served on a church staff . . . and I could hardly bear to raise my head and look in the mirror.

Tears blurred my eyes as I tried to remember the smooth, milk-white complexion I used to have. My fingers twitched, longing to claw at the fiercely itching skin on my face.

I'd tried everything I knew—diets, oatmeal soap, baby oil, vitamins, and enough creams and ointments to fill a small drugstore. And the long line of doctors I'd seen had passed by like a dwindling parade of hope. The rash had only grown worse, and my face swelled, itched, and turned deep tomato-red at the slightest stimulus.

Suddenly the pain behind my eyes tightened as if someone were packing cotton into my sinuses. I reached for a bottle of pain medication and quickly swallowed a couple of pills. I took the maximum of eight pills a day. But they only forestalled the worst of it—when the pain crept down my neck, making clear thinking difficult.

I felt swallowed up by despair, by the long years of this strange affliction. I'd prayed so many times for it to go away. "O God, why don't You help me?"

I dabbed at my eyes and, leaving my secret misery in the bathroom, dressed for work. My head was so sore from the headache, I could hardly pull a comb through my hair. I thought about crawling back into bed. But of course, I couldn't. Actually I liked my work as a third grade schoolteacher. And I had to keep going. I pushed myself into church and community activities.

As I entered school that morning, a little girl peered up at me, her eyes wide with surprise and dismay.

"How come your face looks like *that?*" she asked. (Oh, the blunt honesty of children!)

I raised my hands over my cheeks and tried to explain. But I fell silent. I had no answer.

Not long after that someone told me about a dermatologist at the hospital. I'd seen half a dozen specialists already, but I made an appointment, ready to grasp at anything.

I sat slumped on his examining table after a long series of allergy tests.

"Well, maybe we have an answer," the doctor said. "It appears you are allergic to yourself."

I gazed at him incredulously. "Allergic to myself? You must be kidding!"

"I know it sounds strange, but these allergy tests show you are allergic to your own bacteria."

Hope blew away like the last autumn leaf. Allergic to my own self. How could I escape that?

"We'll make a special serum, using your own saliva," said the doctor, "and teach you how to inject yourself."

And so began the next three years of giving myself shots. The headaches were not quite as severe, nor the rash quite as red— partial relief. The doctor did everything he could, prescribing medicines, creams, and consultations. Still, the ever-present plague was agonizing, embarrassing.

So I followed my old, exhausted pattern and found yet another doctor. This time an outstanding allergist. More tests. More money. He decided I was allergic to a long list of foods, and put me on a diet. For another year I existed on nothing but peas, potatoes, carrots, lettuce, and meat. My weight plummeted to 102 pounds.

"You're wasting away, Mama," said my son one morning, as I dropped my lunch of canned peas in my purse. He was right. Something dreadful was happening to me. And despite it all, the daily headaches persisted and the humiliating rash and acne were splashed across my face big and red as ever. I could no longer even open a box of detergent to do the laundry without my eyes swelling and my skin itching till I was in torment.

This is no way to live, I thought dismally as I draped a scarf across my head and left for work. And worse, there seemed to be no answer at all.

Then one Sunday as I struggled to teach my Sunday school class with a riveting headache, I heard myself saying, "God is the answer." I paused, the echo of my words thundering in my head. As the class continued, the words burrowed inside me like a small, uncomfortable splinter.

After church, I lay on the sofa with a warm cloth across my forehead. I gazed out the broad windows at the tall, silent woods across the road, as the words I'd spoken that morning nudged at me like an unseen elbow. *I am a Christian,* I thought. *I tell other people that God is the answer, that they can find wholeness through Him. Yet I've been a prisoner of this condition for nearly sixteen years.*

Suddenly the familiar old story of the woman in Mark 5:25–34 focused in my mind. The woman who touched the hem of Jesus' robe and was healed. I was so much like her. I, too, had suffered a condition for many years, gone to many physicians, spent nearly all I had to spend, and was not better, but worse. The difference was, the woman in Mark had finally gone to Jesus with faith—and was healed.

Did such healings still happen today? I wondered. If so, could healing really happen to me? There on the sofa, the idea of real healing from God spun in my head. It almost seemed too ancient to be real. If only I could be sure.

The weeks passed and winter melted away. The incredible idea of healing lingered in my mind like a held-over Christmas present. I toyed with the ribbons, afraid to open it, afraid it might turn out empty . . . but strangely, unable to turn away from it.

Then one Sunday, as forsythia framed the world with spring, something happened. I lay in bed trying to find diversion from my headache by watching television. On the screen stood a beautiful young woman—Cheryl Prewitt, Miss America 1980.

"God healed me," she said. "I prepared myself to be healed, and God healed me."

My heart began to pound with a strange excitement. She was speaking to me! No, *God* was speaking to me! He *did* still heal people today.

"Come quick!" I called to my husband and boys. As they hurried to the bedroom, I pointed to the TV where the radiant young woman still spoke. Tears poured down my face. "If God can heal her, then He can heal me," I said.

Finally . . . finally after sixteen desperate years of trying everything else, I was ready to turn to Jesus—as the woman in Mark had done. Again I relived that biblical story in my mind. What was it Jesus had said to her after she had brushed her fingertips across His robe? "Your *faith* has made you whole." And what had Cheryl Prewitt said? "I prepared to be healed by strengthening my *faith.*"

Faith. There was the key. There was what was missing before. My faith had grown flabby, like out-of-shape muscles. I knew intellectually that God is powerful and can heal. But somehow I had to get that knowledge from my mind down into my heart. I had to believe it as fervently as I believed the sun would rise tomorrow.

On May 1, I began to prepare myself for healing like an athlete training for the Olympics. I sat down in the kitchen rocker with a lap full of clean paper and my Bible. I flipped to the concordance in the back—to the headings of healing, health, and faith. I picked out verses, then looked them up, writing each one down word for word on paper. It took a couple of days, but I finally compiled a list of thirty-six Scriptures—sort of a training manual for my faith.

The next day I tucked the papers in my purse. Driving to work, I pulled them out and laid them on the car seat. At the first stoplight I focused on a Scripture, Psalm 103:2–3. "Bless the Lord, O my soul, and forget not all his benefits . . . who healeth all thy diseases," I whispered. I closed my eyes, saying it over and over, letting it sink down inside me. At a stop sign, my eyes fell on another (Jeremiah 17:14). "Heal me, O Lord, and I shall be healed . . ." I said over and over.

All day I kept it up. Before getting out of the car, walking along the school corridors, sitting on the playground at recess. Even in the classroom.

"Children, turn to page two hundred in your math books," I said. As the pages rustled, I looked down at my papers . . . "And he said unto her . . . go in peace, and be whole of thy plague" (Mark 5:34). I repeated it with a prayer for it to sink into my subconscious.

Not a spare moment was lost. By the end of the schoolday my Scripture papers were dog-eared from wear.

I continued my faith exercises throughout the evening. Between stirring a pot and chopping vegetables, I read the verses and meditated on them. At last I put my dog-eared papers on the bedside table and fell asleep, whispering the verse, "If thou canst believe, all things are possible" (Mark 9:23).

In the weeks that followed, this became my constant routine. The papers became attached to me—as inseparable as my own shadow. And by some inexplicable process, the thirty-six Scriptures were slowly sinking into the very core of my being with roots of belief. I was actually beginning to believe—really believe—that I could be healed. I could almost feel my faith stretching and rippling with new strength.

I circled July 12 on the kitchen calendar. "Lord, this is the day I'm asking for complete healing," I said.

Then I added another exercise. I began to visualize my complexion as pink and clear as a newborn baby's and my sinus passages free and well. I imprinted it on my mind day and night. This exercise became rather a strenuous one, because the mirror was such a contrast from my image. The red rash and acne, the throbbing headaches continued. But after a while the image, like the Scriptures, began to sink into the deep believing places of my life. The mirror is wrong, I told myself. Soon it will reflect my inner image.

Late that spring I hurried past a mirror at school. Suddenly I stopped, backed up, and peered into it. I ran my fingers across my face. Was it my imagination or did the fiery red rash seem a bit faded? And my headache. Didn't it seem better today? "Oh, thank You, Lord!" I cried. "You're healing me."

Still I clung to my dog-eared papers, moving through the now well-memorized verses. As my faith deepened and gradually grew stronger, the headaches lessened, and almost imperceptibly my face improved.

July 12 dawned warm and shiny through the bedroom window. I tiptoed to the bathroom mirror, took a deep breath, and peered in. The rash *still* lingered on the lower part of my face and a faint sinus headache tugged behind my eyes. *I will not give up,* I thought. *The day is not over.*

With a sudden burst of faith, I said, "Well, Lord, this is the day! I know it will happen."

As the sun set in an orange glow, I crept to a mirror. As I stared at my reflection, tears sparkled on my face. A face completely smooth and clear. It was the face in my image. The headache of the morning had drifted away as well. Like the woman in Mark, God and faith had made me whole.

For almost a year now I have not experienced another single headache, and my skin remains free and clear. I've gotten rid of all the old ointments, medicines, allergy shots, and diets. The only thing I've kept are my precious dog-eared papers—those powerful Scripture exercises that brought my faith to life. For there's one thing I've learned. While it's important to keep physical muscles strong and well-toned, it's even more important to keep "faith muscles" strong. For they are the ones that churn the spiritual energy, that move the mountains in our lives. Even a mountain like mine, that had towered over me for sixteen years.

A few weeks ago at a meeting, a stranger tapped my shoulder. "Your complexion is so beautiful," she said.

"Oh, thank you," I gasped, my face bursting into an unusually big smile. A smile, I'm sure, no one there really understood . . . except me and God.

Here are the 36 Scriptures Marilyn used:

Proverbs 4:20-22	Mark 9:23	Psalm 91:9,10
Romans 10:17	Mark 11:22–24	Proverbs 3:7,8
Matthew 7:7,11	Luke 6:19	Exodus 15:26
Matthew 8:7,13,17	John 14:13,14	James 5:15
Matthew 9:29,35	Acts 10:38	1 Peter 2:24
Matthew 14:14	Galatians 3:13	Psalm 42:11
Matthew 15:30	John 10:10	Psalm 6:2
Matthew 17:20,21	3 John 2	Psalm 41:4
Matthew 19:2	Hebrews 13;8	Psalm 103:2,3
Mark 1:34	Malachi 4:2	Isaiah 53:4,5
Mark 5:34	Matthew 4:23,24	Jeremiah 17:14
Mark 10:52	Psalm 30:2	1 John 4:4

The Legacy
of Faith

———————————— ❧

What the Heart Holds

William L. Stidger

In the breast of a bulb
Is the promise of spring;

In the little blue egg
Is a bird that will sing;

In the soul of a seed
Is the hope of the sod;

In the heart of a child
Is the Kingdom of God.

Papa Was My Hero

Mary Louise Kitsen

When I was nine years old, I was introduced to my papa!

He was a quiet man who did not talk a lot. Perhaps that is why it took me so long to get to know him. Mama was the one I counted on all day while Papa was off at that mysterious place called "work."

But when he was around, my papa was, in a way, a lot like the street we lived on. Always the same. Our street was a pretty place with trees standing like old giants between the wide street and the narrow, uneven sidewalks. The houses were white, and most had neat black shutters. The front yards were small, and children were advised not to play there. Backyards were for playing. And hanging clothes. Backyards were for gardens and lazy kitty cats and a barking dog. Everyone I knew on my street went to the same church we did. On my street, you felt comfortable because everything stayed the same and you could count on that.

And then the old gentleman next door to us died. His wife was already dead, and they had been childless. So the house was sold. And, at last, that comfortable sameness was shattered. The new neighbors had several children, all noisy and filled with laughter.

Up went colored curtains. (Can you believe that until then I thought curtains only came in white?) The children played in the front yard as well as the back. There was a girl my age, and we soon became good friends. I loved to visit her house. Especially when her father would take out his accordion and play some fast and loud music. I was taught how to polka, quite to the horror of some neighbors who warned my mother that I was certainly headed for trouble. Mama liked the new neighbors, however. Papa did not say much either way. That was like my papa. He was not a talker.

The new neighbors went to a different church. When I asked my mother why they didn't go to our church, she explained that we had freedom of religion in our country.

One Saturday morning the man next door did something that upset some of his neighbors. He painted his front door a bright blue. "That house is becoming an eyesore," one lady told my mother, who was sitting on our front porch.

"If blue suits the Good Lord for His sky, I guess we can live with a blue door," my mother said.

"And what do you say, George?" the lady asked my papa, who was sitting there too, smoking his pipe and reading the morning newspaper. "Aren't you going to do anything about all this? After all, you do live next door to those people."

Papa put his newspaper down and got up. "Yes, I'm going to do something," he said. Mama just smiled. I guess she knew Papa better than I did. Expecting something dreadful to occur, I ran to warn my new friend next door. Together we sat on my back steps worrying. What would my papa do? Could he tell our neighbors to move away? I couldn't imagine my quiet papa doing anything like that. Oh dear!

Suddenly another friend appeared around the corner of my house. "Mary Lou, look what your father's doing!" she commanded. My new friend and I jumped up and ran around to the front. People were looking at the front of my house! My heart was pounding and my legs did not seem to be able to move.

I didn't believe my own eyes!

My papa was painting our front door the same bright blue our newest neighbor had used on his front door.

I walked up to Papa. He turned and looked at me. Then he continued painting. "Remember, child," Papa told me, "if God had intended for everyone to be exactly the same, He would have made them that way. Since He created many different appearances and minds, we must not question these differences."

After the first shock wore off, the new family became just another family. It was pleasant again on our pretty street. Mama declared that Papa had certainly turned the situation around.

I had started looking at Papa with different eyes. I decided he was very brave and very smart.

And then the factory where our new neighbor worked suddenly closed down. It was the time of the Great Depression and jobs were hard to come by. The happy faces and laughter died out next door, replaced by frowns and worried expressions. My friend didn't want to play as much anymore.

One night I started downstairs to get a glass of milk and heard my mama and papa talking about the neighbors. "They can't manage the payment on the house," Mama said, "and they have just about run out of money to buy food. Stanley hasn't found even the hope of work."

Papa had stood by the neighbors before. I decided that he would help them again. There was no doubt in my mind!

It's funny how fast people can change. The same neighbors who had been so opposed to the new family now became involved in their situation. The very next day one of the ladies on our street came to our back door. It was a Saturday and the entire family was still at the breakfast table.

"I'm collecting money to aid our troubled neighbor," the lady said. "How much will you give, George?"

I sat there waiting to see how much my father would give. "Not a cent," my father said. "Charity is not the answer."

I burst into tears and dashed from the room. My heart was broken. I had been so sure that my papa would help the neighbors.

Papa left the house right after breakfast. When suppertime arrived and my papa had not returned home, I decided that Mama must have told him not to come home! I mostly played with my food. How could Papa have done such a terrible thing? Mama looked at me. I looked away. Mama left it alone.

I was in bed when I heard the front door and then my papa's voice. I slipped out of bed and went to the top of the stairs. Mama and Papa were standing in the entryway.

"I had to go all the way to Springfield, but I finally found someone with a job for Stanley. I stopped to tell him before coming on home. He's to start work on Monday."

Springfield? We lived in Connecticut and Springfield was over the state line into Massachusetts! My papa had been traveling all day to find a new job for our neighbor. He hadn't done anything terrible after all . . .

I ran down the stairs and right into my papa's arms! "Oh, Papa," I said, "oh, Papa, I love you."

The job worked out, and a few weeks later the house next door went on sale once again. Papa helped our neighbor load his furniture into the truck he'd borrowed from his new employer.

My friend and I had a tearful good-bye. As the truck went out of view, I held my papa's hand as tightly as I could. "After all that hard work," Papa said, "I could use some ice cream. Why don't you and your mama and me walk down to the ice cream parlor?"

The three of us walked slowly to the center of town. We didn't say much. But then, Papa was never one to talk a lot.

When I was nine years old, I was introduced to my papa. A man who had his own way of being a Christian.

Thank You, Too, Grandpa

Helen Carter

My great-grandfather, whom I called Grandpa, came to live with us when I was eight years old. With him came two battered suitcases and a cardboard box filled with his "valuables." His stay was in-definite—"just till my time has come."

He was short and stocky, with deep blue eyes and sparse gray hair. At a moment's notice his serious face could light up with a quick smile. His hands fascinated me the most. They were unusu-ally small for a man but were thick, callused, and gnarled from heavy work done in his youth. Although those short, powerful hands could wield an ax or sledgehammer with dexterity, they became soft and gentle when he lovingly touched my hair and called me his "girlie."

At the top of the stairway was his room. It was an ordinary room, yet different. There was no bed. Because of an asthmatic condition he slept in a brown leather chair with his feet resting on a footstool. Out of curiosity, I decided to sleep in a chair like Grandpa. No matter how I draped my body in the chair, I found sleeping this way almost impossible. Grandpa never complained.

I found love in his room. His love for me was apparent in many ways, but in this room I learned his great compassion for others. His "valuables" had a story all their own—pleasant memories of the past years. Countless times he leafed through the pages of a faded album, lovingly touching each picture as if he were caressing old friends and loved ones.

His open Bible lay by his chair. It was well worn with penciled markings throughout. The cover was nearly off. One Christmas my grandmother gave him a new Bible. It remained untouched.

The rose and vegetable gardens were Grandpa's private do-main. Here he was a king, a ruler over all of us. His garden flour-ished when others' didn't. "A green thumb he has," our Scottish neighbor said. Grandpa weeded, hoed, and carried water to the thirsty plants. He seemed to nourish each one with tender care. One of his greatest pleasures was to bring us an armload of fresh vegetables or a bouquet of red roses.

Grandpa was almost totally deaf. However, every Sunday morning he sat in the first pew at church, cupping his hand to his ear, trying to hear the sermon. During our cold, wintry weather in Iowa, he never missed a church service. Our pleas for him to stay home instead of going out in the snow were in vain. We would stand at the big dormer windows watching and hoping Grandpa would not slip and fall walking the six blocks home from church. Out of the distance his figure would loom up before us. His head was bent forward against the strong wind and his feet shuffled through the snow. He would enter the door breathing hard, looking at us with those blue eyes as if to say, "See, I made it."

At night I often crept down the hall and sat crouched outside the door to hear his prayers. He prayed long and aloud, always beginning with the same words, "Lord, thank You for my blessings." I would wrap my nightgown around my legs to keep warm in the cold hall and stay until his prayers were finished.

Back in my warm bed I pondered his words, "Lord, thank You for my blessings." Being old, deaf, sleeping upright in a chair, with no worldly goods, what blessings could he have? Yet, night after night I listened to his prayers and I knew one blessing he did have. He had faith.

One evening in late summer, we came home to find Grandpa's crumpled body lying at the foot of the stairs. His left arm and shoulder were dangling by his side. On his face were cuts and bruises. Grandpa had fallen down the stairs. He looked at me and I could almost hear him say, "Girlie, my time has come."

It seemed odd to see Grandpa lying in a big four-poster bed. Somehow, he didn't look the same. His arm was bandaged; his face was pale, and his breath came in short gasps. Soon he left us.

Although we tried, the garden and the roses never looked the same again. The green thumb was gone. The gardens seemed to know it too.

After he was gone, I sat in his big leather chair many times. I missed him, as did the box of "valuables," the old photograph album, and his well-worn Bible. Sometimes at night I can still hear his voice saying his prayers, opening with the same words, "Lord, thank You for my blessings."

Many years have passed since I lived in the same house with Grandpa. The example of his life, set before me during my childhood days, is with me still. When problems arise and my path seems impassable, I remember to be thankful for my many blessings, to love and to have faith.

Thank you, Grandpa, for helping me remember again.

Crossroads

Romuald Spasowski

On the afternoon of Saturday, December 19, 1981, I sat at my desk in my residence in Washington, D.C., facing the most difficult decision of my life. The Solidarity movement in my native Poland was being crushed. A week before, martial law had been declared. In my mind's eye there were images of half-frozen Poles facing tanks, gas, cannon, and clubs with only their bare hands. Some miners had been killed. It was more than I could stand.

At the age of sixty, I was about to complete my second assignment as ambassador of Poland to the United States. The time had come for me to retire, to go back to my homeland, back to an uncertain future. Why uncertain? Because I knew I could not live peacefully or honestly in a country where the ideology was no longer one I believed in. On this day, at this hour, I had to choose between going back or seeking political asylum in the United States.

As I struggled with my decision, my eyes fell on two familiar objects on the desk before me. One was a bronze statue; the other, a little brown book. I had inherited the little statue from my father. Called "The Dying Gladiator," it was a sculpture of an ancient Gaul lying on his shield, sword fallen from his hand. Father had always kept the gladiator on his desk at our family home in Warsaw. As a scholar and idealist, Father was a strong antifascist. He believed that communism offered equal rights to all people and that Poland would at last be free of the kind of exploitation that it had been forced to endure for centuries. And as an atheist, he believed in materialism, the philosophy that the only values and objectives of mankind are to be found in the material world.

I remembered how he would hold the bronze figure and explain that, to him, the gladiator symbolized man's continuing fight against injustice. "If one must die in the battle," he said, "let it be a gallant death with honor."

The little brown leather-covered book was worn, its pages dog-eared. I picked it up, and as I thumbed through its pages, that long-ago day when my grandmother gave it to me came back with startling clarity. I was a nineteen-year-old who had joined the Polish

Army to fight the Nazi invasion. Our unit had been scattered by Stuka dive bombers and I had picked my way across the ravaged countryside to Volhynia, where our forces would reorganize.

Hungry and exhausted, I stumbled into the outskirts of our family estate, Lityn. My grandmother Sumowska was still living there! I hadn't seen her in years. I found her little house and knocked on the wooden door. It slowly creaked open, and there she was, Babcia, smaller, frailer than ever. "Romek, wnuczek [little grandson]!" she cried out, and with tears streaming down her wrinkled cheeks, she began kissing me.

She gave me food and I slept until evening. Then, in a low-ceilinged, raftered room, we sat at an old oak table and talked. The light from the oil lamp was soft and the war seemed far away. The gleaming brass samovar muttered in a rolling boil, and a servant girl put a loaf of home-baked rye bread, fresh butter, *twarog* cheese, and smoked boar ham on the table.

Grandmother smiled at me from across the table, her brown eyes twinkling in the lamplight.

"Babcia," I sighed, "when I was a little boy, you used to keep treasures in a wooden trunk. Do you still have that trunk?"

She nodded, and we rose to go to her bedroom, where the large trunk, covered with a dark spread, stood in a corner. As I opened it, I felt like a child again. I culled through beautifully embroidered tapestries and an ebony box of letters my ancestors had written and received over the ages. One, on frayed yellow paper, was from King Jan Sobieski III (1629–1696) warning an ancestor of the Turkish menace and signed simply "Jan, the King."

Grandmother handed me crosses, silver shields with images of the Virgin. Then she reverently picked up a little brown book.

"You see this prayer book?" she said softly, referring to it in Polish as *ksiazeczka do nabozenstwa*. "It's called the 'little Dunin' because it was put together by your ancestor Marcin Dunin, archbishop of Gniezno and Poznan, who died about a hundred years ago. It has served me for many, many years."

She leaned forward with it. "Do you want this *ksiazeczka* as a keepsake?"

"No," I quickly answered, "I'm an atheist, Grandmother."

"Yes, yes," she sighed slumping back in her chair. "That is how your father raised you. But who knows, the time may come when you'll think differently."

I quickly changed the subject, saying, "It seems our ancestors had been well educated."

"Yes," she said, "to the east and south of us, past the Styr and Stochod rivers, their blood has been shed for centuries. Perhaps when you're old enough, everything that was meant to flow in your veins will return to you . . ."

She trailed off as we sat in silence. Early the next morning as I prepared to leave, she thrust the little brown book at me. "Take the little Dunin," she urged. "Someday you'll learn to pray. The time will come, Romek," she nodded knowingly, "when you will find that it will give you the strength you need.

"At least," she smiled, "it will help you remember your old Babcia."

The war went on. I suffered the death of my father who took his life rather than be a prisoner of the Nazis. I saw Poland crushed. My life brightened, however, when I fell in love with green-eyed, blonde Wanda, so intelligent except for the fact that she was an ardent Christian believer. Despite what I considered her old-fashioned beliefs, we married in the church and were blessed with a daughter, Misia, and a son, Kaytus.

Then came a mixed peace, with the Soviet Union dominating my country. I advanced in the Polish Communist government, earning diplomatic appointments and honors. Yet the Poland I loved sank deeper and deeper under Soviet repression. And I began to see the vast abyss between my father's idealism and the harsh reality of communism.

From time to time as I chafed at party bureaucracy, my mind would drift back to that warm evening with my grandmother, and I would pick up her little prayer book. One day I began to read it. Eventually, I became intrigued with the idea of a loving God who offered us eternal life through His Son, Jesus Christ.

Wanda, noting my interest, handed me her small *Nowy Testament*. "It might help you, Romek," she offered.

It did, for I began to see that Christianity was what communism promised but never delivered. In fact, I read that the first people to accept Christ were the very people the communists believed they appealed to most—the poor, the workers, the oppressed.

I thought of Poland invaded by the Nazis and Soviets in 1939, of the thousands killed and deported, of my friends murdered, of our priests being persecuted. And as I continued reading the Bible and Babcia's little prayer book, my faith burned stronger.

And so I came to the crossroads of that December afternoon. I faced an agonizing choice: return and live in material comfort but with sealed lips, or face an unknown future in the United States and speak out for my people.

I sat at my desk studying the two symbols of my heritage, the bronze gladiator and the little brown prayer book. "The time has come for truth," I said to Wanda, standing up. Then, with a trembling hand, I picked up the phone to call the U.S. State Department to ask for political asylum. The receiver seemed as heavy as the weight of my sixty years as I faced the awesome reality of what I was about to do. Then I knew this was that hour my grandmother spoke of when, in handing me the little prayer book, she had said, "The time will come, Romek, when you will find that it will give you the strength you need."

Editor's note: *When he decided to stay in the U.S. in 1981, Romuald Spasowski was the highest-ranking diplomat ever to defect from a communist country. On April 9, 1985, he was baptized by John Cardinal Krol in Philadelphia.*

Miss Jenny's Sunshine

Ora Lindsay Graham

It was the end of a warm spring Monday at our house on Pine Street. I had washed and hung out clothes all morning, baked a cake, cut out a dress . . . along with the usual hustle four kids create. Now they were bathed and ready for bed. They jumped back and forth on their trundle beds as I struggled with clean sheets and pillow cases. I wanted to just crawl in with them and sleep forever, I was so tired. But their father would be home soon and I knew it would be hours before I could collapse into the comfort of my own bed.

The children kept playing and singing, rehearsing their prayers, "Now I lay me down to sleep." *The sheets are getting thinner,* I thought, and made a mental note to be more frugal so I could buy new ones. A change without having to wash would be nice.

I reached for the last one and suddenly the sweet, clean smell of Miss Jenny's sheets filled my head. I pressed the one I was holding close to my face to smell again that special aroma of those sheets that I could never forget.

Memories flooded over me. Miss Jenny Cole. I had not thought of her in years. She was Iris's mother, and Iris was my best friend. I wondered what ever had happened to her and to Iris, whom I had loved so dearly as a child.

Our days in the little country schoolhouse when we were ten years old I remembered as a time of complete joy and never a problem. Iris was always happy and she had a short little nose with exactly thirty-one freckles across it. I counted them one day. I had too many to count. During recess we chased each other and played hide and seek. When Iris got hot, her dark red hair kinked in ringlets round her face and sweat glistened in the curls. I wanted her curly hair and she wanted long thick braids like mine. She wanted my blue eyes, I wanted her brown ones, and we giggled a lot because we each wanted to be the other.

Sometimes we'd sit under the schoolhouse during lunch and tell each other secrets, things we shared with no one else. Often I'd swap my apple for her ham biscuit or a baked potato for some pie.

Iris lived with her mother and her three-year-old brother, Danny, about seven miles down Highway 19. Miss Jenny's husband was killed at a train crossing when he was just thirty years old. Miss Jenny worked a vegetable garden and raised chickens and took in sewing for their livelihood. On Saturdays she, Iris, and Danny came to my father's store and he always bought Miss Jenny's chickens and clean fresh eggs. Papa said he never bought a dirty egg from her in his life.

Miss Jenny, tall and slender, pulled her black hair straight back into a tight bun; her face looked pinched by its force. Browned from the sun, her skin was smooth and clean. She didn't smile a lot, but when she did smile her whole face glowed. She was not pretty. She was handsome and wholesome. Lots of men wanted to court her, Papa said, but she took no thought of anyone but God, Iris, and Danny.

Usually in the spring Mama let me spend the night with Iris, and I so loved going there. We got off the school bus at Remus Cemetery. The church had blown away five years before in a storm and the Coles had been coming to our church ever since. It was at least a half mile through the woods and pasture to their house, but cows and kids had made a good walking trail.

As we left the thicket of pine trees, the little frame house, brown from age and weather, came into view. It was a beautiful silhouette upon the hill as the sun set, making the house, cows, dogs, fences, trees, and barn look like cardboard cutouts placed on a grassy knoll. We could see the clean white sheets waving from the clotheslines, and the mules in the pasture raised their heads from grazing to calmly look us over.

The chickens scattered in the yard, squawking loudly as Danny came running—mumbling and laughing—to meet us. Iris dropped her books, ran to meet him, and they embraced, giggling as she kissed him again and again. "I love you," she would say, holding his face close to her own. Then he'd hug me, too, and we'd walk the rest of the way hand in hand.

Miss Jenny wore white starched aprons when she cooked, and I never saw a spot of food on one of them. Her talk was always serious unless something unusual happened, like the time an old settin' hen got after Iris and me for trying to hold one of her baby chicks. She laughed about it.

Learning was important to Miss Jenny. "If you don't study," she'd say as we pondered our homework, "you won't learn, and if you don't learn, you'll grow up ignorant like me, and I'm not having that. My Iris and Danny must work with their heads, not their hands."

Then she would laugh such a lovely laugh. I thought it was sad that she didn't laugh more often.

We were put to bed at eight o'clock at night. About 8:30 I remember seeing the shadows move in the room as Miss Jenny entered with a kerosene lamp in one hand and the Bible in the other. I lay very still, and I can still smell the sunshine in the clean white sheets I lay upon.

She placed the lamp on a table and, standing at the foot of the bed, she read from the Bible. I don't remember what she read, but it was from the word of God.

Then Iris slowly slid to her knees and Miss Jenny knelt and placed her arm around her. She prayed for Iris's safety; that she would be a good girl and obey all of God's laws. Iris then made her own requests. She thanked God that He had let me come to visit, and for little Danny.

Miss Jenny moved to my side, and I, too, slid to my knees and felt her arm fold gently around me and heard her pray. It was more real to talk to God in that little room than in any church sanctuary I've ever seen. I felt as if I were in His arms.

Danny moved to the side of his bed and waited for his mother to remove her arm from around him before he arose.

I whispered to Iris, asking how Danny knew what was happening, that he was so little and didn't know much. She said she'd tell me if I promised not to tell a living soul. I promised faithfully.

"Well, when Papa died, Mama took me and Danny to the cemetery and we sat beside Papa's grave and Mama just lifted up her arms to Heaven—"

She stopped and turned to me. "You better promise me again you won't tell this 'cause I've told no one before."

"I won't tell, Iris. I promise." She held my hand as I crossed my heart under the cover and hoped to die if I told.

"Well, anyway, Mama just lifted up her arms to Heaven and she said, 'God, I can't do it by myself. Can't raise the children by myself. I got nobody but You, so today I'm giving them to You. Iris and Danny. I'm giving them to You so my burden won't be so powerful!' "

Iris giggled. "Don't you see? Mama gave us to God. That's how come He takes such good care of us. That's how come Danny understands 'bout praying and things."

I envied her. My mother had not given me to God. But Iris reminded me it wasn't necessary since Papa was still alive.

Now, more than twenty years later, it was as if Miss Jenny's sunshine had come to live with me! I was so filled with homesickness for her, that little house and Iris, that I sat on the bed, the crumpled fresh-washed sheet close in my arms, and cried.

That night I knelt in prayer with each of my children and offered them to God.

As I closed their door behind me I thought. *Oh, Miss Jenny, did you wish for new sheets, too? And did your legs ache as mine do tonight . . . were you ever so tired?* Of course. Her burdens had been powerful, but I had only smelled the sunshine and heard her pray, and then always slept soundly in Miss Jenny's house.

Lighting the Path

Josephine Millard

He who carries a candle of joy
   Will light the path for a brother
And furnish the spark to start the flame
   Of hope in the heart of another.

A NOTE TO THE READER

This original Guideposts book is brought to you by the same editors who prepare *Guideposts*, a monthly magazine filled with true stories of people's adventures in faith.

If you have found inspiration in this book, we think you'll find monthly help and inspiration in the exciting stories that appear in our magazine.

Guideposts is not sold on the newsstand. It's available by subscription only. And subscribing is easy. All you have to do is write Guideposts Associates, Inc., Carmel, New York 10512. For those with special reading needs, *Guideposts* is published in Big Print, Braille, and Talking Magazine.

When you subscribe, each month you can count on receiving exciting new evidence of God's presence and His abiding love for His people.